101 SONGS FOR EASY GUITAR BOOK 3

Wise Publications
London / New York / Sydney

Published by
Wise Publications
14-15 Berners Street, London, W1T 3LJ, UK.

Exclusive distributors:
Music Sales Limited
Distribution Centre, Newmarket Road, Bury St Edmunds,
Suffolk, IP33 3YB, UK.

Music Sales Pty Limited
20 Resolution Drive, Caringbah,
NSW 2229, Australia.

Order No. AM960278
ISBN 0-7119-7719-4
This book © Copyright 1980, 1991 Wise Publications,
a division of Music Sales Limited.

Compiled and designed by Pearce Marchbank and Peter Evans.

Printed in the EU.

Your Guarantee of Quality:
As publishers, we strive to produce every book
to the highest commercial standards.

The music has been freshly engraved and the book has been
carefully designed to minimise awkward page turns and to make
playing from it a real pleasure. Particular care has been given
to specifying acid-free, neutral-sized paper made from pulps
which have not been elemental chlorine bleached.

This pulp is from farmed sustainable forests and
was produced with special regard for the environment.

Throughout, the printing and binding have been planned
to ensure a sturdy, attractive publication which should give
years of enjoyment.

If your copy fails to meet our high standards, please inform us
and we will gladly replace it.

www.musicsales.com

Anarchy In The UK

Words and music by Johnny Rotten, Paul Cook, Steven Jones and Glen Matlock

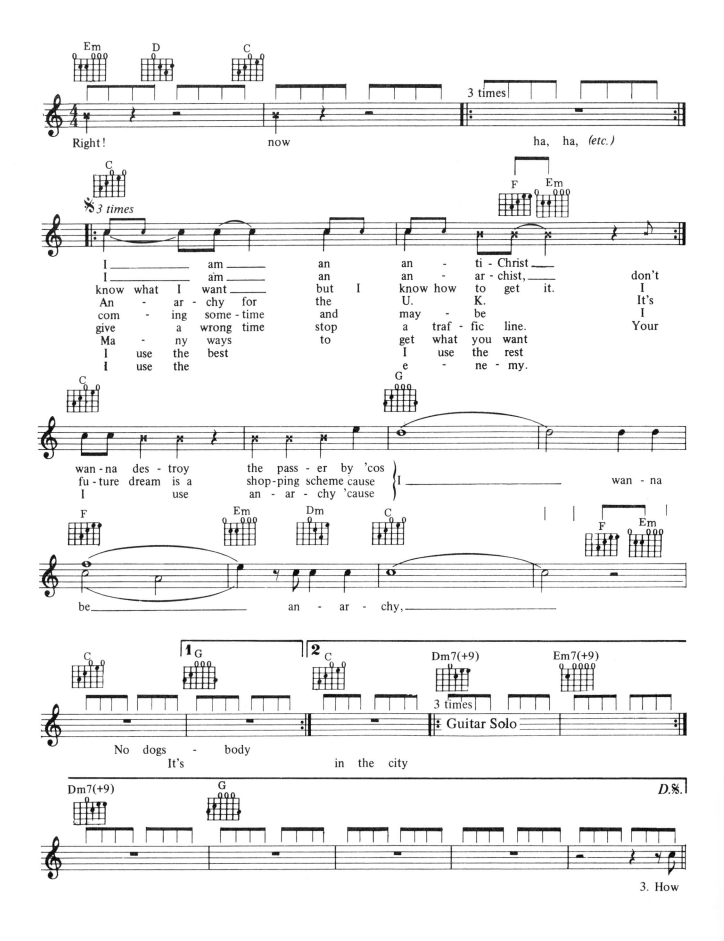

Its the only way to be

Is _____ this ____ the M. P. L. A. _____ or
is _____ this ____ the U. D. A. _____ or _____ thought ___ it was the
is _____ this ____ the I. R. A. _____ I

U. _____ K. ____ or just _____ an

oth - er _____ coun - try _____

Another council tenancy.

I _____ wan - na be _____

____ an an - ar - chist _____ (get _____

(Oh what a name) And

pissed des - troy.)

5

God Save The Queen

Words and music by Johnny Rotten, Paul Cook, Steven Jones and Glen Matlock

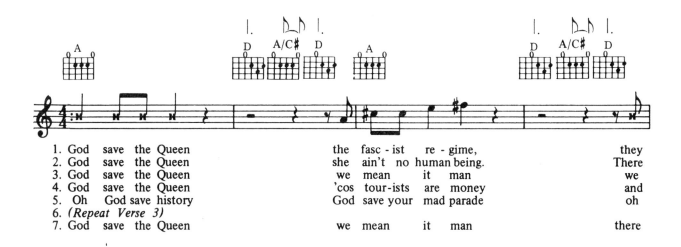

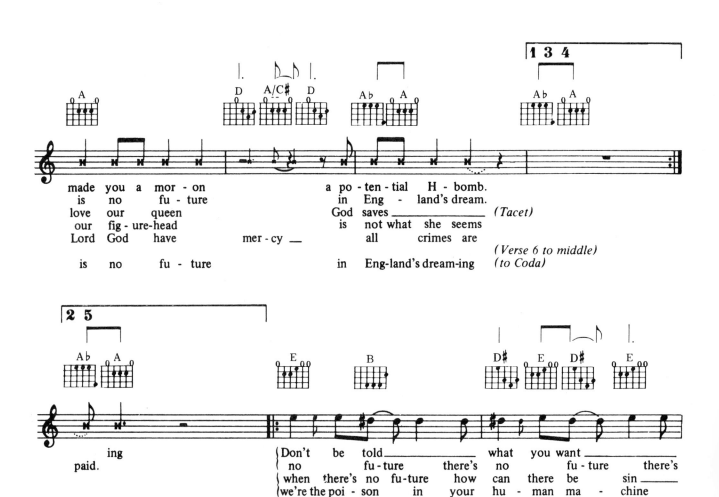

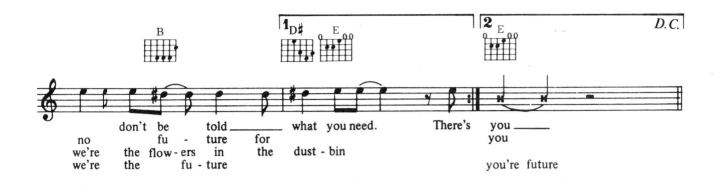

don't be told _____ what you need. There's you _____

no   fu - ture for

we're the flow-ers in the dust-bin

we're the fu - ture

you

you're future

MIDDLE

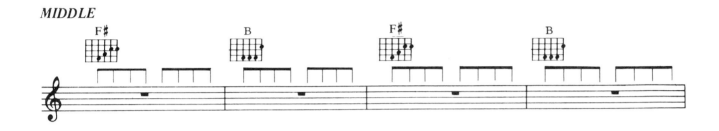

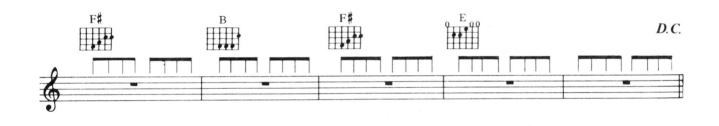

CODA

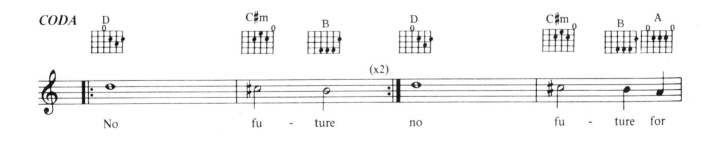

No   fu - ture no   fu - ture for

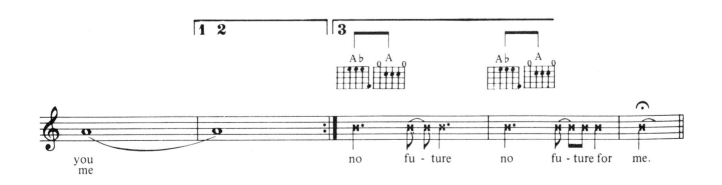

you

me

no fu - ture no fu - ture for me.

7

Pretty Vacant

Words and music by Johnny Rotten, Paul Cook, Steven Jones and Glen Matlock

Guitar
4 times

add Drums
4 times

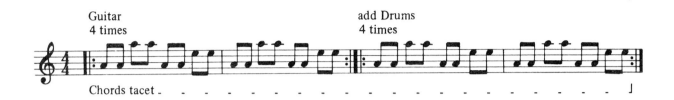

Chords tacet

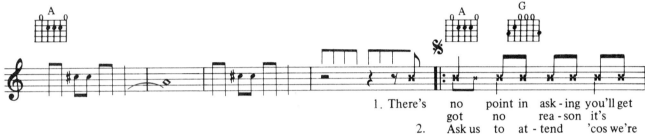

1. There's no point in ask-ing you'll get
   got no rea-son it's
2. Ask us to at-tend 'cos we're
   Don't be-lieve il-lus-ions 'cos
3. *Repeat verse 1*

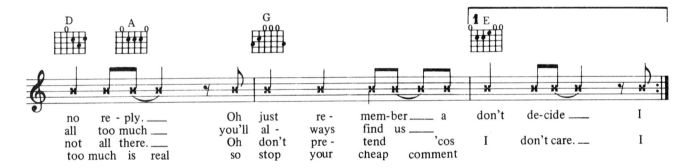

no re-ply. ___ Oh just re- mem-ber ___ a don't de-cide ___ I
all too much ___ you'll al - ways find us ___
not all there. ___ Oh don't pre- tend 'cos I don't care. ___ I
too much is real so stop your cheap comment

out to lunch
'cos we know what we feel

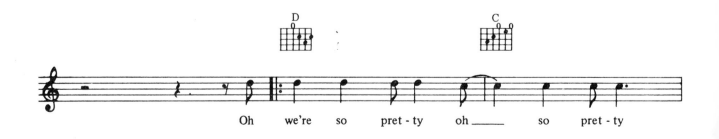

Oh we're so pret-ty oh ___ so pret-ty

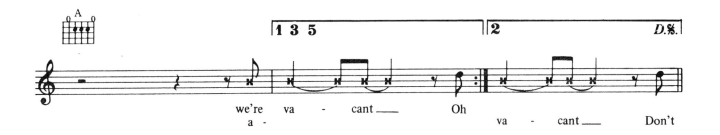

we're va - cant ___ Oh va - cant ___ Don't
a -

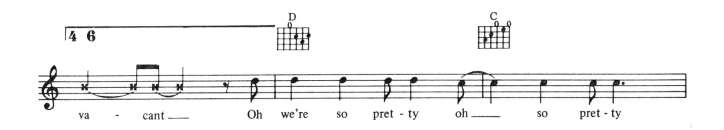

va - cant ___ Oh we're so pret - ty oh ___ so pret - ty

Ah but now

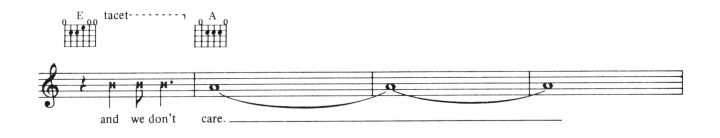

and we don't care. ___

There's We're pret - ty ___

a- pret-ty va - cant. ___ We're we don't care. ___

Hanging On The Telephone
Words and music by Jack Lee

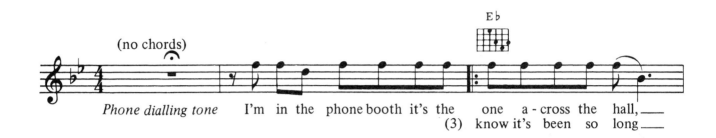

11

Call Me
Words and music by Deborah Harry and Giorgio Moroder

Col - or me,__ your col - or, ba - by, col - or me,__ your car.__

Col - or me,__ your col - or, dar - ling,

I know who__ you are.__ Come up off__ your col -

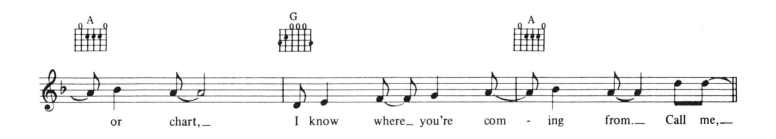

or chart,__ I know where__ you're com - ing from.__ Call me,__

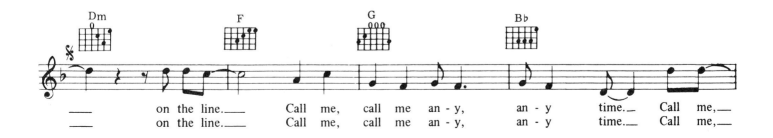

on the line.__ Call me, call me an - y, an - y time.__ Call me,__

on the line.__ Call me, call me an - y, an - y time.__ Call me,__

Oo, _____ he speaks_ the lan - guag - es_ of love. ____ .

Oo, _____ a - mo - re, chia - ma - mi_ *chia-ma-mi*

Oo, _____ ap - pel - moi, mon___ che - rie,___ ap - pel - moi. An - y time_

___ an - y place,_ an - y - where,___ an - y - way. _____ An - y time,_

___ an - y place,_ an - y - where,_ an - y day. _____ Call me, _

___ on my line._ Call me, call me an - y, an - y time._ Call me,_
___ on my line._ Call me, call me and a sweet de - sign. Call

___ for a ride._ Call me, call me for some o - ver - time._ Call me,_
me, call me, for your lov-er's lov-er's al - i - bi._ Call me,_

15

Atomic

Words and music by Deborah Harry and Jimmy Destri

17

Walking On The Moon

Words and music by Sting

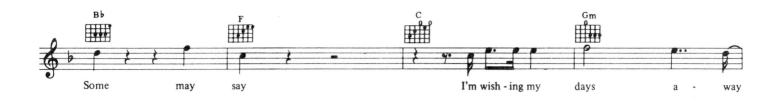

Some may say   I'm wish-ing my   days   a - way

___ no way   and if it's the   price   I   pay__

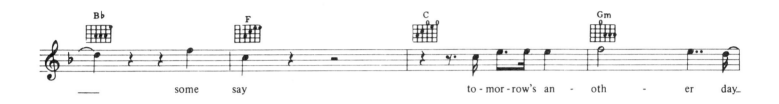

___ some say   to - mor-row's an - oth - er day_

To Coda ✛

___ you'll stay   I may as well play

D.C. al Coda

✛ *CODA*   *Repeat to fade*

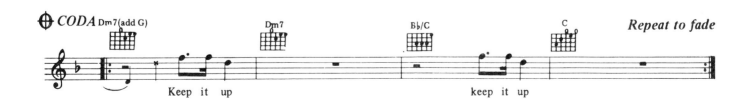

Keep it up   keep it up

The Bed's Too Big Without You

Words and music by Sting

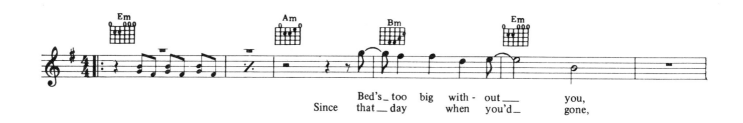

Since that __ Bed's_ too big with - out __ you,
day when you'd __ gone,

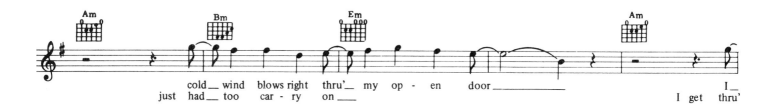

cold __ wind blows right thru'_ my op - en door _____ I _
just had __ too car - ry on ___ I get thru'

___ can't sleep_ with your mem - 'ry night _ Made love to
___ day but __ late at night _

dreaming dreams of what used to be _ when she left I was
my pil - low __ but it didn't feel right _ ev - 'ry day

cold in - side ____ that look _ on my
just the same old rules_ for the

face   was___ just   pride___   no   re -
same   old___ game

- grets   no   love no   tears   liv - ing on my own   was the
gained   was heart - ache   all I   made   was

least   of my___ fears___   Now the Bed's   too   big with - out___   you,___   the
one mis - take___   bed's   too   big with - out___   you,___   the

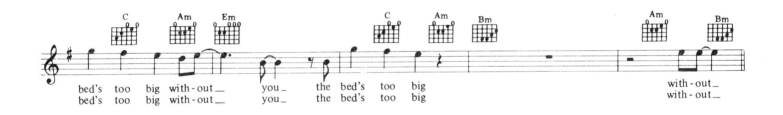

bed's   too   big with - out___   you___   the bed's   too big   with - out___
bed's   too   big with - out___   you___   the bed's   too big   with - out___

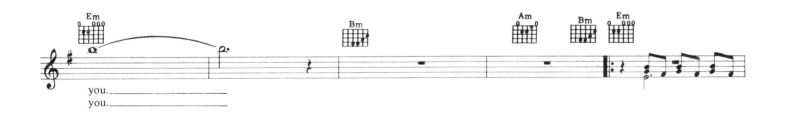

you.___
you.___

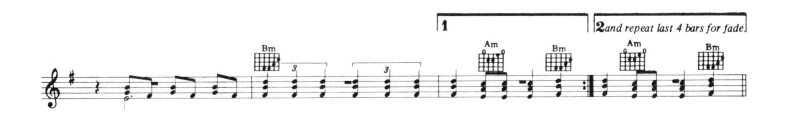

So Lonely
Words and music by Sting

Reggae feel

Well some-one told me yes-ter - - day
Now no-one's knocked up - on my door

that when you throw your love a - - way
for a thou - sand years or___ more

You act as if you just don't care you
all made up and no-where to go

look as if ___ you're ___ go - ing some - where ___ But
wel - come to ___ this ___ one man ___ show ___ Just

I just can't con - vince my self I could - n't live with
take a seat they're al - ways free no sur - prise no

no - one ___ else. And I can on - ly
mys - ter - y. In this theat - re that I

23

Roxanne
Words and music by Sting

Moderately fast

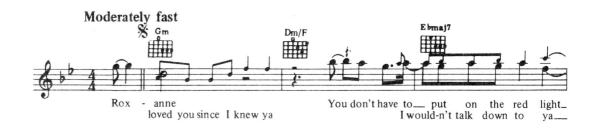

Rox - anne
loved you since I knew ya
You don't have to— put on the red light—
I would-n't talk down to ya—

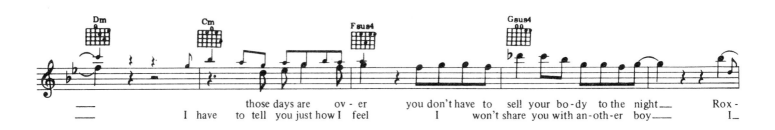

— those days are ov - er you don't have to sel! your bo-dy to the night— Rox-
— I have to tell you just how I feel I won't share you with an-oth-er boy— I—

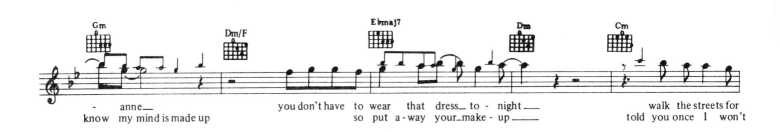

- anne— you don't have to wear that dress— to - night— walk the streets for
know my mind is made up so put a-way your_make-up — told you once I won't

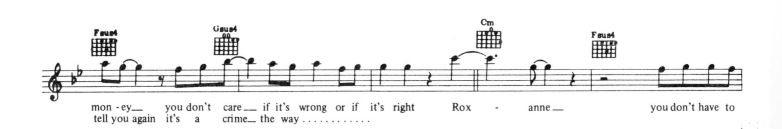

mon - ey— you don't care— if it's wrong or if it's right Rox - anne— you don't have to
tell you again it's a crime— the way . . . .

24

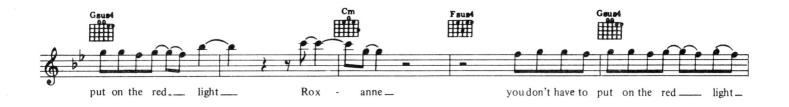

put on the red light — Rox - anne — you don't have to put on the red light —

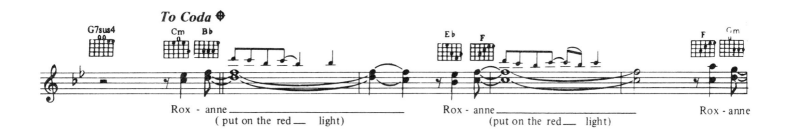

Rox - anne (put on the red light) Rox - anne (put on the red light) Rox - anne

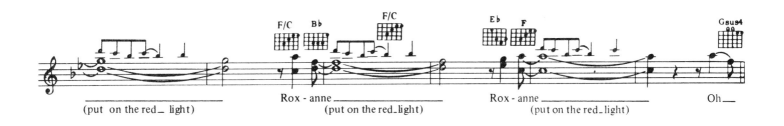

(put on the red light) Rox - anne (put on the red light) Rox - anne (put on the red light) Oh —

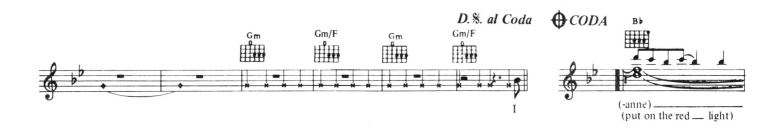

(-anne) (put on the red light)

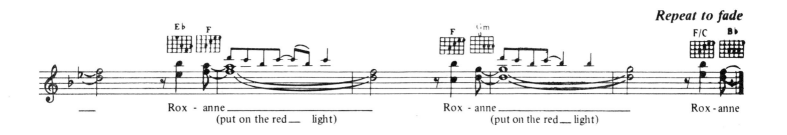

Rox - anne (put on the red light) Rox - anne (put on the red light) Rox - anne

Message In A Bottle

Words and music by Sting

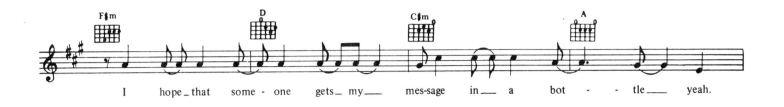

I hope _ that some - one gets _ my _ mes-sage in _ a bot - - tle _ yeah.

mes-sage in _ a bot - - tle _ yeah.

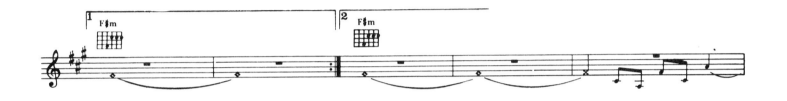

mes-sage in _ a bot - - tle _

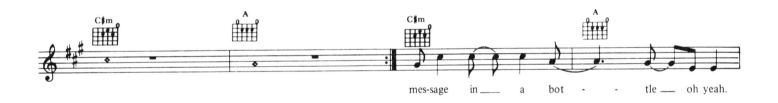

mes-sage in _ a bot - - tle _ oh yeah.

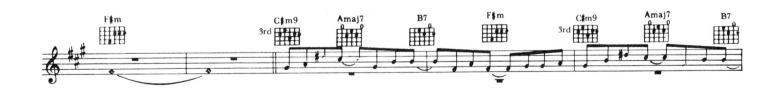

I'm send - ing out _ an S. _ O. S. _ I'm

27

Somethin' Else

Words and music by Ed Sheeley and Eddie Cochran

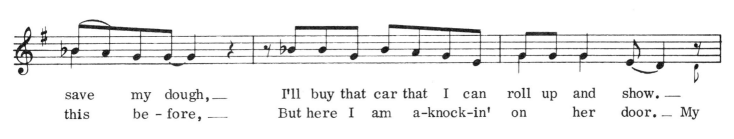

3. Hey look-a here, ___ Just wait and see, ___ Work hard ___ and
4. Look-a here, ___ What's all this? ___ Nev-er thought I'd do

save my dough, ___ I'll buy that car that I can roll up and show. ___
this be - fore, ___ But here I am a-knock-in' on her door. ___ My

Get me that girl and we'll go rid-ing a - round, ___ We'll look real ___ sharp with a
car's out front and it's all mine, It's a for-ty-one ___ job not a

white down, ___ I keep right on a-dream-in' and a - think-in' to my-self,
fif - ty-nine, ___ I got that girl and I'm a - think-in' to my-self,

If it all comes true man, ___ She's somethin' else.
She's fine look - in' man, ___ She's somethin' else.

29

C'Mon Everybody

Words and music by Eddie Cochran and Jerry Capehart

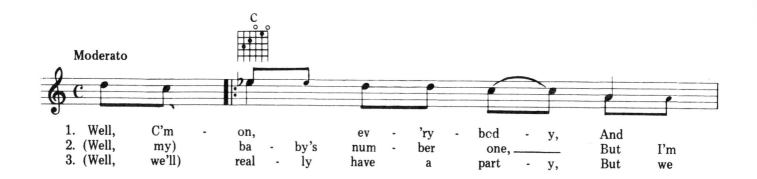

1. Well, C'm - on, ev - 'ry - bod - y, And
2. (Well, my) ba - by's num - ber one, But I'm
3. (Well, we'll) real - ly have a part - y, But we

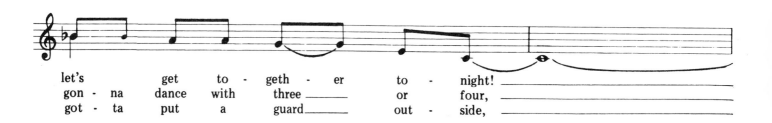

let's get to - geth - er to - night!
gon - na dance with three or four,
got - ta put a guard out - side,

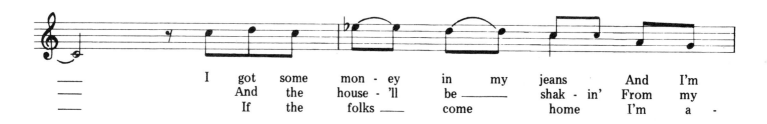

— I got some mon - ey in my jeans And I'm
— And the house - 'll be shak - in' From my
— If the folks come home I'm a -

real - ly gon - na spend it right!
bare feet slap - pin' the floor.
- fraid they gon - na have my hide.

Been   a   do - in'   my   home   work
When   you   hear _____ that   mus - ic   you
There'll be   no _____ more   mov - ies   for   a

all   week   long,   Now   the   house   is   emp - ty,   the
just   can't   sit   still.   If   your   broth -   er   won't   rock   then   your
week   or   two;   No   more   run - nin'   a -   round   with   the

(Shout)

folks   are   gone.   *Oo,   oo!*
sis -   ter   will.   *Oo,   oo!*   C'm -
us - u - al   crew.   *Who   cares.*

- on,   ev - 'ry - bod - y!

1 & 2   3

2. Well,   my
3. Well,   we'll

31

Cut Across Shorty

Words and music by Marijohn Wilkin and Wayne P. Walker

al - so had the looks, But
Short - y far be - hind, And
tur - tle and the hare, When

Short - y must - a had some - thing, boys, That
Short - y heard him hol - ler out, "Miss
Dan crossed over the fin - ish line, He

can't be found in books.
Lu - cy you'll soon be mine." "Cut a - cross,
found Short - y wait - ing there.

Short - y, Shorty cut across," That's what Miss Lu - cy

said, "Cut a - cross, Short - y, Shorty cut across, It's

1 & 2

3

you I want to wed." 2. Now wed."
3. But

Three Steps To Heaven
Words and music by Bob and Eddie Cochran

Step two ———— she falls with you. ————

Step three ———— you kiss And hold her tight - ly, ——————— Yeah! that

1

sure seems like Hea - ven to —— me.

2

D. 𝄋

The me. ——————— Just fol - low

steps one, two and three.

Milk Cow Blues
Words and music by John Estes

Moderately slow

Well, I woke up this morn - in', looked out of the door

I can tell that was my Milk Cow by the way that she lows; If you see my Milk Cow,

Please send 'er on home. Ain't

had no milk and but - ter, Since my cow's been gone.

Well, you got to treat me right, day by day, Get

out your lit - tle prayer book, Get down on your knees and pray, 'Cause you're gon - na

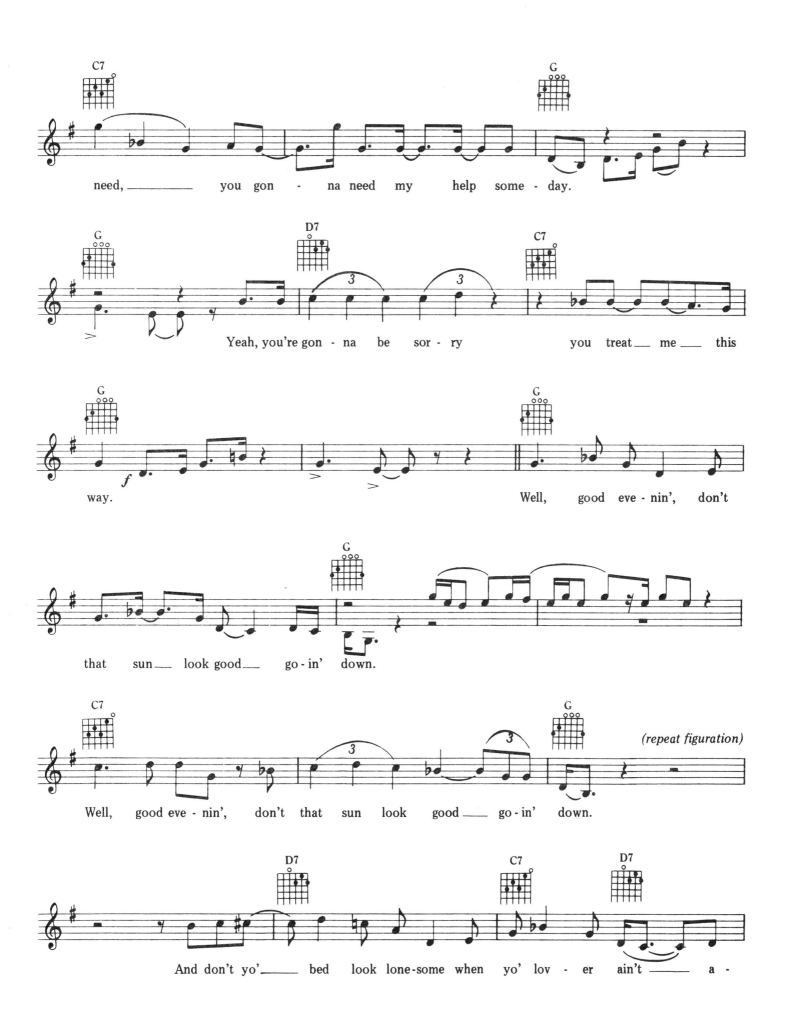

need, _____ you gon - na need my help some - day.

Yeah, you're gon - na be sor - ry you treat ___ me ___ this

way. Well, good eve - nin', don't

that sun ___ look good ___ go - in' down.

(repeat figuration)

Well, good eve - nin', don't that sun look good ___ go - in' down.

And don't yo' _____ bed look lone - some when yo' lov - er ain't _____ a -

round.

I've tried ev-'ry-thing, ba-by, to

get a-long___ with you, Now I'm gon-na tell you what I'm___ gon-na do; I'm

gon-na stop my___ cryin', leave___ you a-lone; You don't think I'm leav-in', just

count the days I'm gone, 'Cos you're gonna need___ me,___ Need your lov-ing daddy one of these

days.___ You're gon-na be sor-ry that

you treat-ed me this way._____

The Long Run

Words and music by Don Henley and Glenn Frey

1. I used to hur - ry a lot. I used to wor - ry a lot. I used to

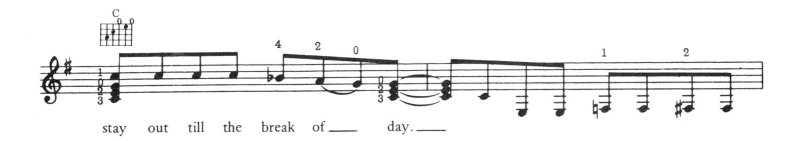

stay out till the break of ___ day. ___

Oh, that did - n't get it. It was high time I quit it. I just

could - n't car - ry on that ___ way. ___

Oh, I did some dam - age, I know it's true. ___ Did - n't

39

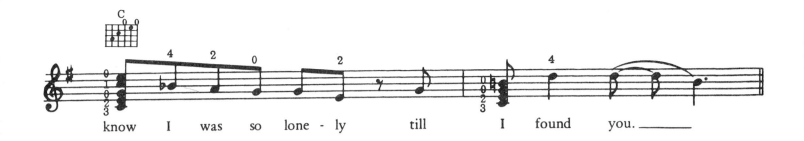

know I was so lone - ly till   I   found   you. _____

You can go the dis - tance.   We'll find out ____ in the   long __ run __ (in the

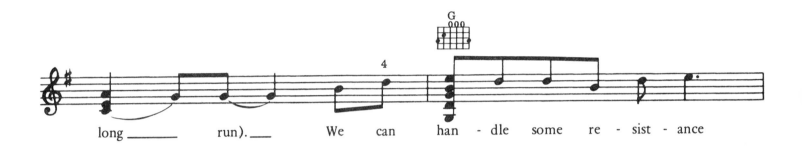

long _____ run). __   We   can   han - dle some re - sist - ance

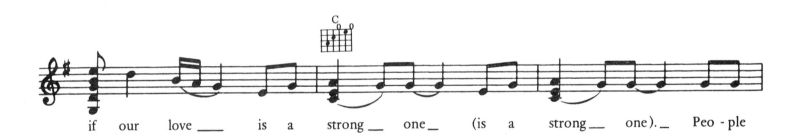

if   our love ___ is a strong __ one __ (is a strong __ one). __ Peo - ple

talk - in' a - bout us.   They   got   noth - in' else to do.   When it

all goes down_   we will still come through _ in the long ___ run. __

Ooh, I want to tell ___ you, it's a long ____ run. ___

1.

2. *D. S.* 𝄋 *(instrumental) and fade*

2. You know, I

Additional lyrics

2. You know, I don't understand why you don't treat yourself better,
Do the things, the things that you do.
'Cause all the debutantes in Houston, baby,
Couldn't hold a candle to you.
Did you do it for love? Did you do it for money?
Did you do it for spite? Did you think you had to, honey?
Who is gonna make it? We'll find out
In the long run (in the long run).
I know we can take it if our love
Is a strong one (is a strong one).
Well, we're scared, but we ain't shakin'.
Kind of beat, but we ain't breakin'.
In the long run. Ooh, I want to tell you,
It's a long run.

Heartache Tonight

Words and music by Don Henley, Glenn Frey, Bob Seger and J. D. Souther.

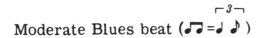

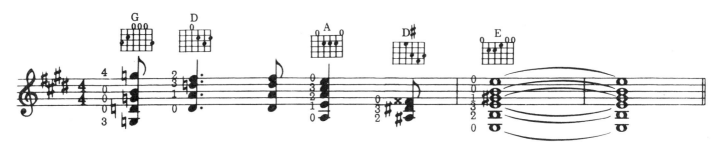

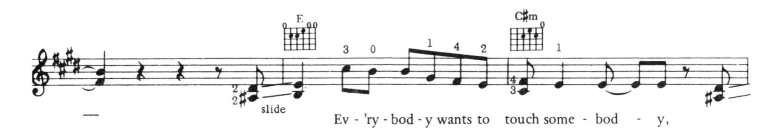

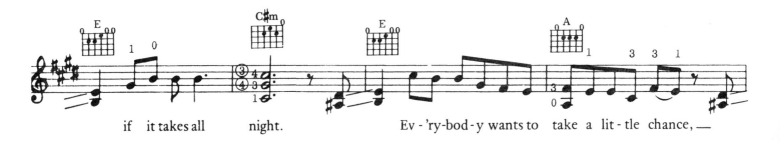

heart - ache to-night,   a heart - ache to-night,   I   know.

There's gon - na be a heart - ache to-night,   a heart - ache to-night,   I

To Coda ⊕

know.   Lord, I know.   Some peo-ple like to stay out late. _

Some folks can't hold out that   long.   But no - bod - y wants to

go home now; _   there's too much go - in'   on.

This night is gon - na last for - ev - er.   Last all, last all   sum-mer

long.   Some time be - fore the   sun comes   up, _

43

the ra-di-o is gon-na play that song. _____ There's gon-na be a

heart - ache to-night, a heart - ache to-night, I know.

There's gon-na be a heart - ache to-night, a heart - ache to-night, I

know. Lord, I know. There's gon-na be a heart - ache to-night. The

moon's shin - in' bright, so turn out the light, and

we'll get it right. There's gon - na be a heart - ache to - night, _____ a

heart - ache to-night, I know.

The Last Resort
Words and music by Don Henley and Glenn Frey

Slowly, in 2

1. She came from Prov - i - dence, the one in Rhode Is - land, where the old world shad - ows hang heav - y in the air. She packed her hopes and dreams like a ref - u - gee, just as her fa - ther came a - cross the sea.

Repeat and fade

2. She heard about a place people were smilin'.
   They spoke about the red man's way, and how they loved the land.
   They came from everywhere to the Great Divide,
   Seeking a place to stand or a place to hide.

3. Down in the crowded bars, out for a good time,
   Can't wait to tell you all what it's like up there.
   And they called it Paradise. I don't know why.
   Somebody laid the mountains low while the town got high.

4. Then the chilly winds blew down across the desert,
   Through the canyons of the coast, to the Malibu,
   Where the pretty people play, hungry for power,
   To light their neon way and give 'em things to do.

5. Some rich men came and raped the land; nobody caught 'em.
   Put up a bunch of ugly boxes, and Jesus, people bought 'em.
   And they called it Paradise, the place to be.
   They watched the hazy sun sinking in the sea.

6. You can leave it all behind and sail to Lahaina,
   Just like the missionaries did so many years ago.
   They even brought a neon sign: "Jesus is coming."
   They brought the white man's burden down. They brought the white man's reign.

7. Who will provide the Grand Design? What is yours and what is mine?
   There is no more new frontier; we have got to make it here.
   We satisfy our endless needs and justify our bloody deeds
   In the name of destiny and in the name of God.

8. And you can see them there on Sunday morning.
   Stand up and sing about what it's like up there.
   They call it Paradise. I don't know why.
   You call some place Paradise, kiss it goodbye.

New Kid In Town

Words and music by Don Henley, Glenn Frey and John David Souther

Moderately

1. There's talk on the street; — it sounds so fa - mil - iar.

Great ex - pec - ta - tions, ev - 'ry-bod - y's

watch - in' you. ___ Peo - ple you meet, —

___ they all seem to know you. E - ven your

old — friends treat you like you're some - thin' new. ___

Johnny-come-late - ly, the new kid in town.

Ev-'ry-bod-y loves_you, so don't_ let them down. ___

when you're not a - round? _____

There's so man - y things you should have told _____ her.

But night af - ter night you're will - ing to

hold _ her, just hold _ her. Tears _ on your shoul - der.

There's talk on the street; it's there to re - mind you

that it does-n't real-ly mat - ter which side you're on. ____

You're walk-in' a - way, and they're talk-in' be - hind you.
They will

nev - er for-get you till some-bod - y new comes a - long. __

Where you been late - ly? ____ There's a new kid in town. __

Ev - 'ry-bod-y loves_him. (Don't they?) Now he's hold-ing her, and you're still a -

round. Oh, my my. __ There's a new kid in

50

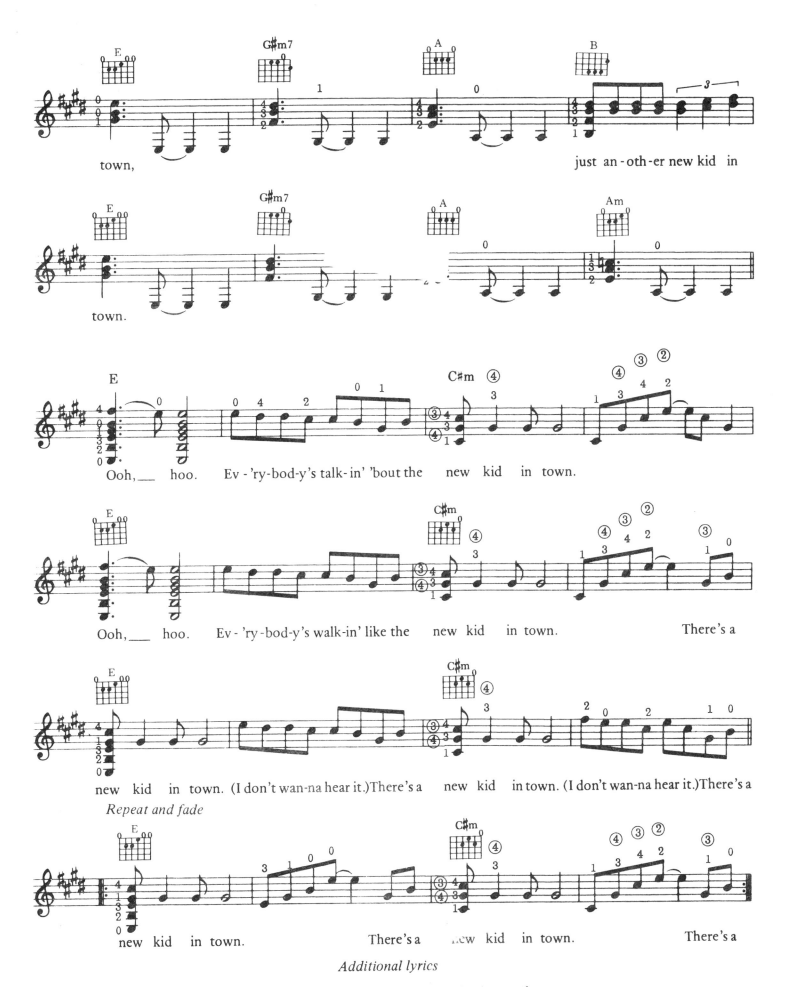

town,   just an-oth-er new kid in

town.

Ooh, ___ hoo. Ev-'ry-bod-y's talk-in' 'bout the new kid in town.

Ooh, ___ hoo. Ev-'ry-bod-y's walk-in' like the new kid in town.   There's a

new kid in town. (I don't wan-na hear it.)There's a new kid in town. (I don't wan-na hear it.)There's a

Repeat and fade

new kid in town.   There's a new kid in town.   There's a

Additional lyrics

2. You look in her eyes; the music begins to play.
   Hopeless romantics, here we go again.
   But after a while, you're lookin' the other way.
   It's those restless hearts that never mend.
   Johnny-come-lately, the new kid in town.
   Will she still love you when you're not around?

51

Life In The Fast Lane

Words and music by Don Henley, Glenn Frey and Joe Walsh

Moderate Rock beat

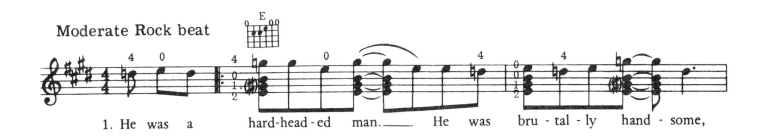

1. He was a hard-head-ed man.___ He was bru-tal-ly hand-some,

and she was ter-mi-nal-ly pret-ty.

She held him up, and he held her for ran-som in the

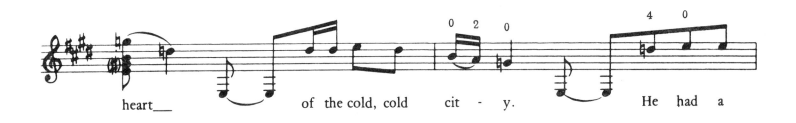

heart___ of the cold, cold cit-y. He had a

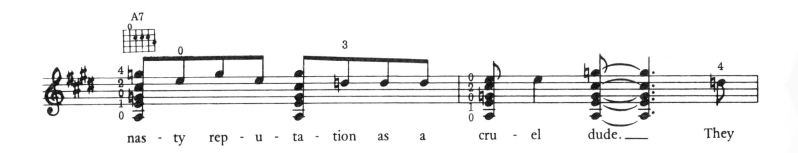

nas-ty rep-u-ta-tion as a cru-el dude.___ They

said he was ruth - less; they said he was crude.— They had

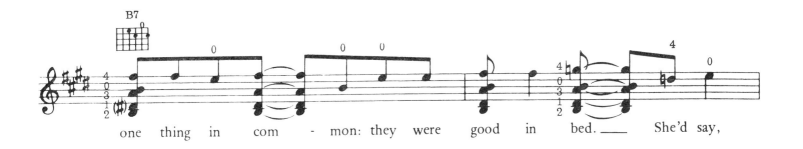

one thing in com - mon: they were good in bed.___ She'd say,

"Fast - er, fast - er. The lights are turn - in' red."

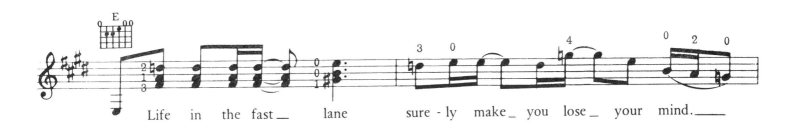

Life in the fast_ lane sure - ly make_ you lose_ your mind.___

Life in the fast_ lane.

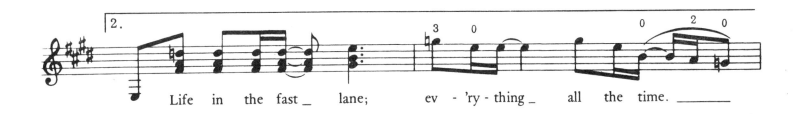

Life in the fast _ lane; ev-'ry-thing _ all the time. _____

Life in the fast _ lane. Life in the fast _ lane;

ev - 'ry-thing _ all the time. _____ Life in the fast _ lane.

Repeat and fade

E

Additional lyrics

2. Eager for action and hot for the game,
   The coming attraction, the drop of a name.
   They knew all the right people; they took all the right pills.
   They threw outrageous parties; they paid heavily bills.
   There were lines on the mirror, lines on her face.
   She pretended not to notice; she was caught up in the race.
   Out every evenin' until it was light,
   He was too tired to make it; she was too tired to fight about it.
   Life in the fast lane *(etc.)*

3. Blowin' and burnin', blinded by thirst,
   They didn't see the stop sign; took a turn for the worst.
   She said, "Listen, baby. You can hear the engine ring.
   We've been up and down this highway; haven't seen a goddamn thing."
   He said, "Call the doctor. I think I'm gonna crash."
   "The doctor say he's comin', but you gotta pay him cash."
   They went rushin' down that freeway; messed around and got lost.
   They didn't know they were just dyin' to get off.
   And it was life in the fast lane *(etc.)*

Free Man In Paris

Words and music by Joni Mitchell

Suggested right hand pattern:

Moderately fast

"The way I see it," he said, "you just can't
dream - ers and tele - phone

win it.
scream - ers;

Ev - 'ry - bod - y's in it for their own __
late - ly I won - der what I do it

gain; you can't please 'em __ all. There's al - ways
for. If I had my __ way I'd just

some - bod - y call - in' you down. I do my
walk through those doors and wan - der

best and I do a good bus' - ness. There's a lot - a peo - ple
down the Champs É - ly - sées, go - ing ca - fé to

ask - in' for my_____ time. They're try'n' to get a -
cab - a - ret think - ing how I'll feel when I

head; they're try'n' to be a good friend of mine. _____
find that ver - y good friend of mine. _____

I was a

free man in Par - is, I felt un - fet - tered and a - live. _____

56

There was no-bod-y call-in' me up for fa-vors and no one's

fu-ture to de-cide.___ You know, I'd go back there to-

mor-row but for the work I've tak-en on,___ stok-in' the

star-mak-er ma-chin-'ry be-hind the pop-u-lar songs."___

1.

2.

___ "I deal in

Big Yellow Taxi
Words and music by Joni Mitchell

Suggested right hand pattern:

Moderate Rock beat

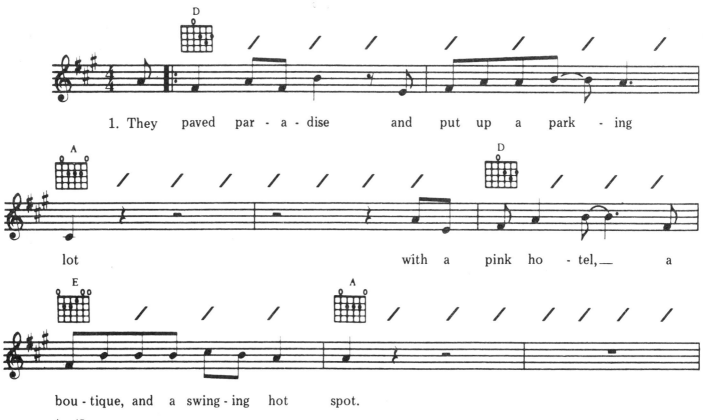

1. They paved par - a - dise and put up a park - ing

lot with a pink ho - tel, ___ a

bou - tique, and a swing - ing hot spot.

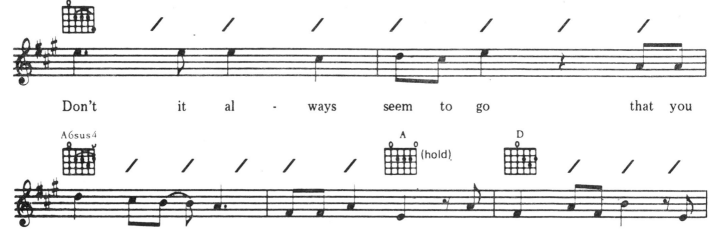

Don't it al - ways seem to go that you

don't know what ___ you've got till it's gone? They paved par - a - dise and

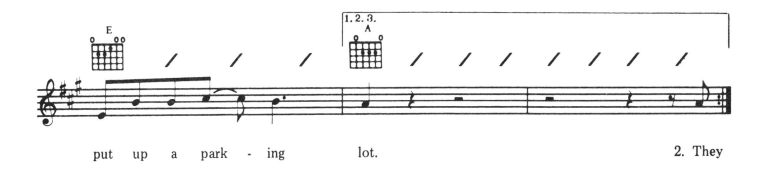

put   up   a   park   -   ing   lot.   2. They

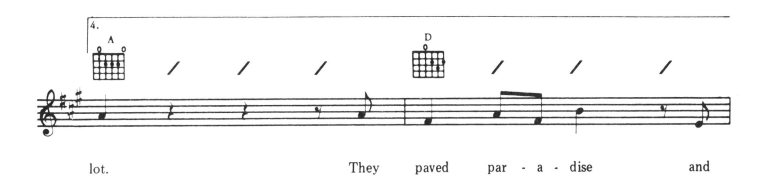

lot.   They   paved   par   -   a   -   dise   and

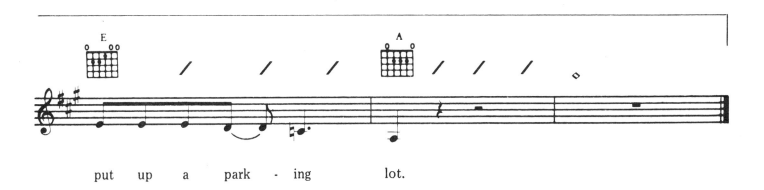

put   up   a   park   -   ing   lot.

2. They took all the trees and put them in a tree museum,
  And they charged all the people a dollar and a half just to see 'em.
  Don't it always seem to go that you don't know what you've got till it's gone?
  They paved paradise and put up a parking lot.

3. Hey, farmer, farmer, put áway that D.D.T. now.
  Give me spots on my apples but leave me the birds and the bees, please!
  Don't it always seem to go that you don't know what you've got till it's gone?
  They paved paradise and put up a parking lot.

4. Late last night I heard the screen door slam,
  And a big yellow taxi took away my old man.
  Don't it always seem to go that you don't know what you've got till it's gone?
  They paved paradise and put up a parking lot.
  They paved paradise and put up a parking lot.

Slow Dancer
Words and music by Jack Tempchin

Slowly

I have nev - er loved __ a la - dy,

nev - er touched __ a silk - en knee. __ Ma - con ba - by,

you drove me cra - zy; you were so eas

y to me.

Lay me down _____ in Geor - gia pine __ cones, whis - per to me
Nev - er see _____ your face in sun - light, moon-light sends you

Don't Let It Bring You Down

Words and music by Neil Young

Slowly, in 2

Old man ly - in' by the side of the road__ with the
Blind man run - ning through the light of the night__ with an

lor - ries roll - ing by,____ blue moon sink - ing from the
an - swer in his hand,____ come on down to the

weight of the load__ and the build - ings scrape the sky.___
riv - er of sight__ and you can real - ly un - der - stand.___

Cold wind rip - ping down the al - ley at dawn__ and the morn - ing pa - per
Red lights flash - ing through the win - dow in the rain, can you hear the si - rens

flies, ___ dead man ly - ing by the side of the road__ with the
moan? ___ White cane ly - ing in a gut - ter in the lane if you're

day - light in his eyes.
walk - ing home a - lone. } Don't let it bring you down,___ it's

on - ly cas - tles burn - ing; find some - one who's turn - ing, and

you will come a - round.___

Don't let it bring you down, it's on - ly cas - tles

burn - ing; just find some - one who's turn - ing and

1. you will come a - round.___

2.

Like A Hurricane
Words and music by Neil Young

1. Once I thought I saw — you in a crowd - ed, ha - zy bar, —
2. I am just a dream - er, but you are just a dream, —

— dan - cing on — the light — from star to star. —
— and you could have — been an - y - one to me. —

— Far a - cross the moon -
— Be - fore that mo - ment you touched —

beams, I know that's who you are. — I
my lips, that per - fect feel - ing when time just slips a -

saw your brown eyes turn - ing once — to fire. —
way be - tween — us and our fog - gy trips. —

Additional lyric

3. You are just a dreamer and I am just a dream,
And you could have been anyone to me.
Before that moment you touched my lips,
That perfect feeling when time just slips away between us
and our foggy trips.

Chorus

65

Walk On
Words and Music by Neil Young

I can't tell ____ them how to feel. ____

____ Some get stoned, _____ some get

strange; _____ soon - er or lat - er it

all gets real. Walk on, _____

walk on, _____ walk

on, w_-_k on. _____

Repeat and fade

67

King Creole
Words and music by Jerry Leiber and Mike Stoller

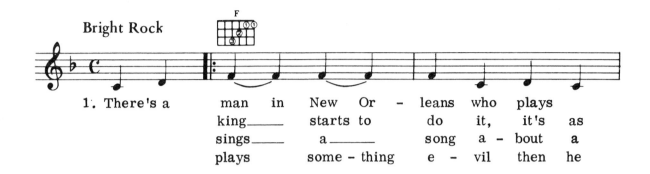

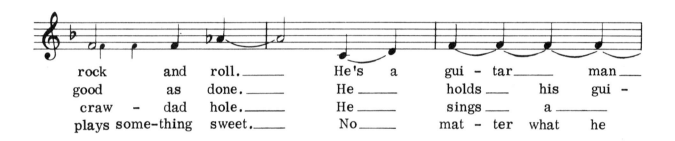

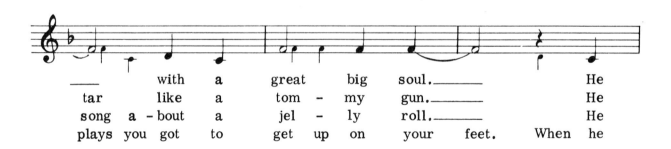

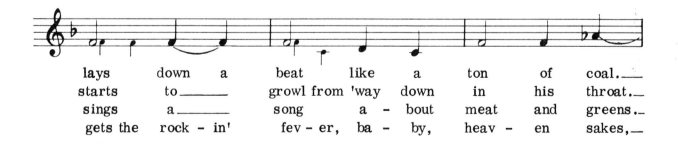

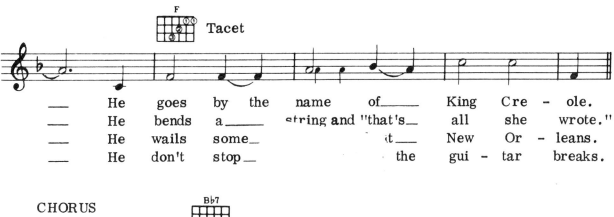

He goes by the name of____ King Cre - ole.
He bends a____ string and "that's__ all she wrote."
He wails some____ it___ New Or - leans.
He don't stop __ the gui - tar breaks.

CHORUS
Tacet

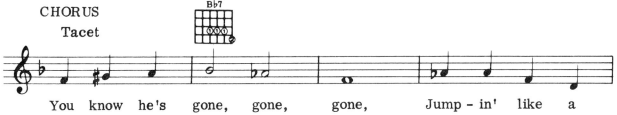

You know he's gone, gone, gone, Jump - in' like a

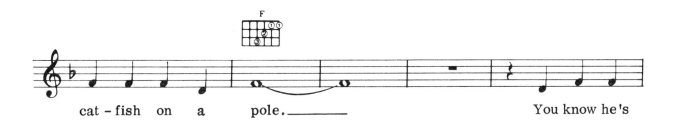

cat – fish on a pole._____ You know he's

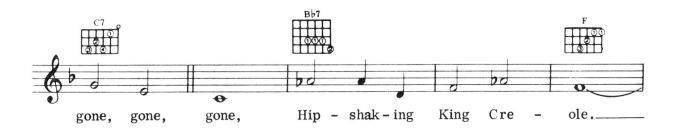

gone, gone, gone, Hip - shak - ing King Cre - ole._____

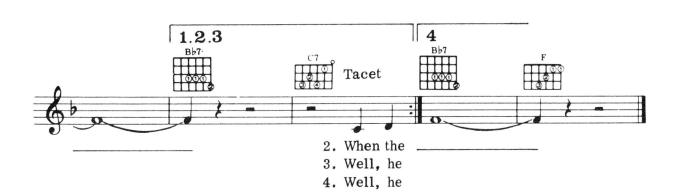

_____

2. When the _____
3. Well, he
4. Well, he

A Big Hunk Of Love

Words and music by Aaron Schroeder and Sid Wyche

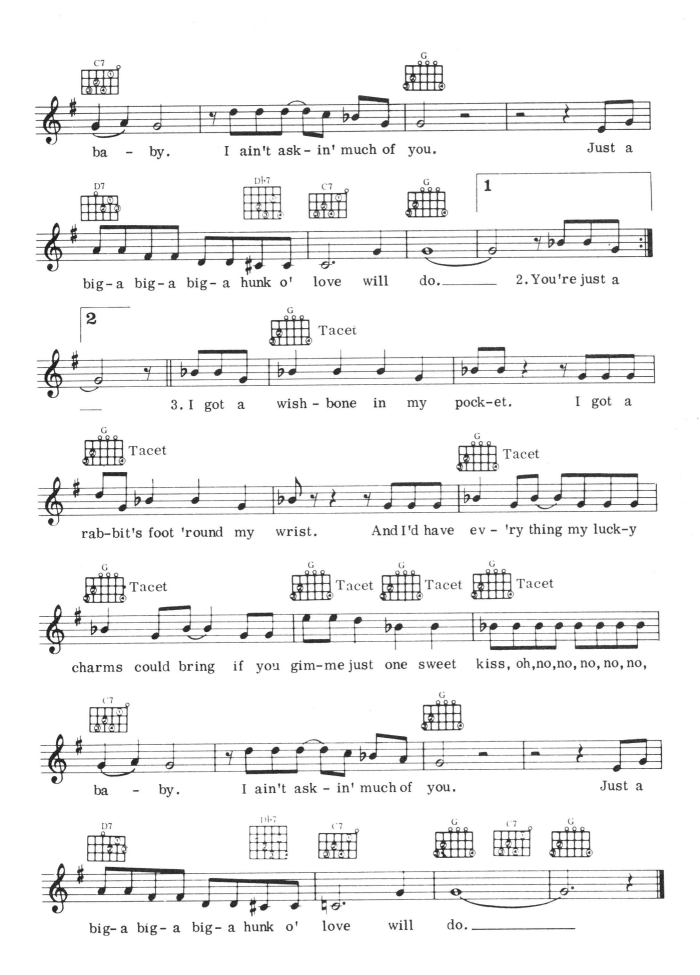

ba - by.   I ain't ask - in' much of you.   Just a

big-a big-a big-a hunk o' love will do._____ 2. You're just a

__   3. I got a   wish - bone in   my   pock-et.   I   got a

rab-bit's foot 'round my   wrist.   And I'd have ev - 'ry thing my luck-y

charms could bring if you gim-me just one sweet   kiss, oh, no, no, no, no, no,

ba - by.   I ain't ask - in' much of you.   Just a

big-a big-a big-a hunk o' love   will   do._____

Long Tall Sally

Words and music by Enotris Johnson, Richard Penniman and Robert Blackwell

Bright Rock tempo

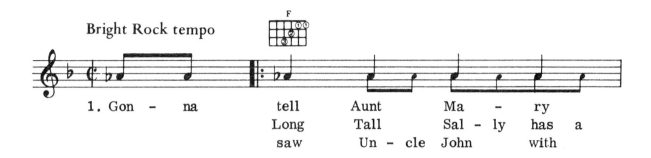

1. Gon - na tell Aunt Ma - ry
Long Tall Sal - ly has a
saw Un - cle John with

'bout Un - cle John, He says he has the blues, But he
lot on the ball, And no - bod - y cares if she's
Long Tall ___ Sal - ly, He saw Aunt Ma - ry com - in' And he

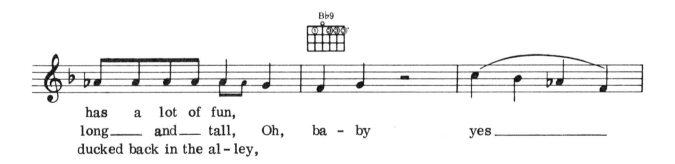

has a lot of fun,
long ___ and ___ tall, Oh, ba - by yes ___
ducked back in the al - ley,

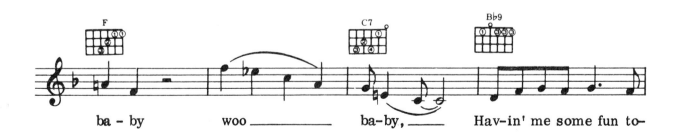

ba - by woo ___ ba - by, ___ Hav - in' me some fun to-

night.__ yeah!__ 2. Well, yeah!__ we're gonna have some fun to-night,
3. Well I

__ Gon-na have some fun to-night__ woo!__ We're gon-na

have some fun to-night,__ Ev-'ry-thing will be all right.

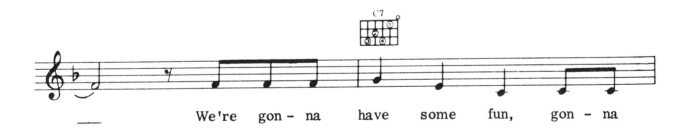

__ We're gon-na have some fun, gon-na

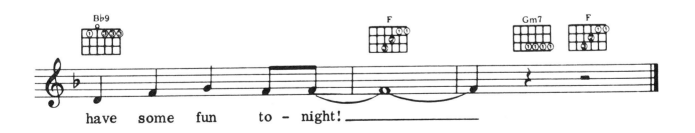

have some fun to-night!_____

Mean Woman Blues

Words and music by Claude DeMetrius

Medium Rock

I got a wo-man mean as she can be.

I got a wo-man mean as she can be.

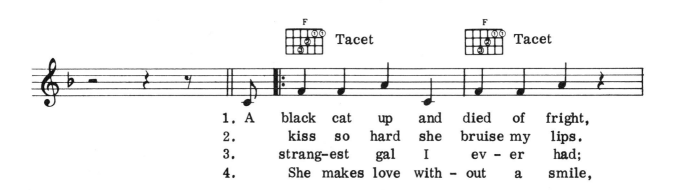

Some-times I think she's al-most mean as me,

Tacet   Tacet

1. A black cat up and died of fright,
2.   kiss so hard she bruise my lips.
3.   strang-est gal I ev-er had;
4.   She makes love with-out a smile,

Tacet

'Cause she crossed his   path last night.
Hurts so, good my   heart just flips.
Nev – er   hap – py   'less she's mad.
Ooh hot   dog, that   drives me   wild.

Oh,   I   got   a   wo – man

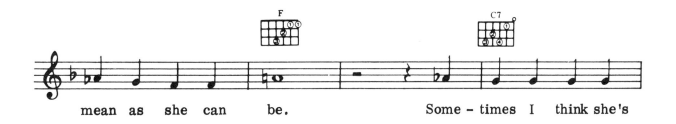

mean   as   she   can   be.   Some – times I   think she's

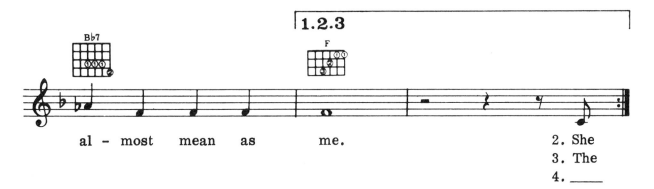

1.2.3

al – most   mean   as   me.   2. She
                                                    3. The
                                                    4. _____

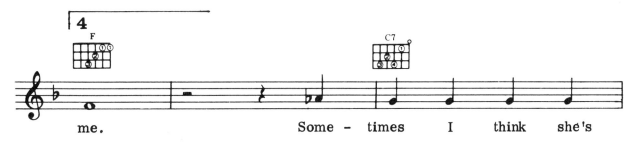

4

me.   Some – times   I   think   she's

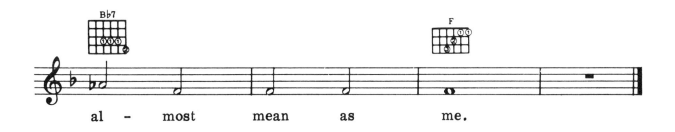

al –   most   mean   as   me.

Paralyzed

Words and music by Otis Blackwell and Elvis Presley

Bright shuffle

CHORUS

When you looked in-to my eyes, _____ I
When we kissed, ooh, what a thrill. _____ You

stood there_ like I was hyp-no-tized _____ You
took my hand and ooh, ba-by what a chill. _____ I

sent a feel-ing to my spine, a feel-ing warm and
felt like grab-bin' you real tight, squeeze and squeeze with

smooth and fine, But all I could do was stand there par-a-
all my might, But all I could do was stand there par-a-

1. lyzed. _____
2. lyzed. _____ Oh, yah, luck-y me, I'm

sing-in' ev-'ry day, _____ Ev-er since that

day you came my way, _____ You made my life for
me just one big hap-py game. I'm gay ev-'ry morning, at
night I'm still the same. Do you re-mem-ber that won-der-ful
time _____ You held my hand and swore that you'll be
mine? _____ In front of the preacher you said, "I do!" I
couldn't say a word for think-ing of you. All I could do was
stand there par-a-lyzed. _____ lyzed. _____

Red House
Words and music by Jimi Hendrix

min - ute, some - thing's wrong, ba - by. The key won't un - lock the door. ___

I got a bad, bad feel - ing that my ba - by don't live here no

more. I might as well go on back down, ___

go back 'cross yon - der o - ver the hill.

I might as well go back o - ver yon - der way back o - ver yon - der 'cross the

hill. (That's where I come from) 'Cos if my ba - by don't love me no more ___

I know her sis - ter will! ___

Are You Experienced

Words and music by Jimi Hendrix

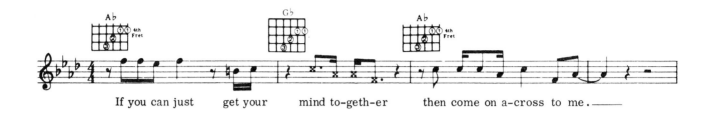

If you can just get your mind to-geth-er then come on a-cross to me.

We'll hold hands _ an' then we'll watch the sun rise from the bot-tom of the sea.

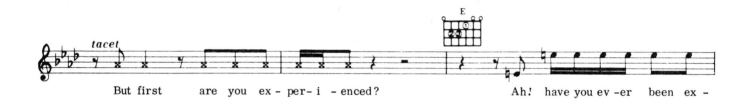

But first are you ex - per - i - enced? Ah! have you ev -er been ex -

per-i -enced? _ Well, _ I have. _ I know, I know _

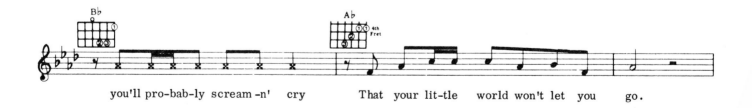

you'll pro-bab-ly scream -n' cry That your lit-tle world won't let you go.

But who in your meas-ly lit-tle world   are you trying to prove that   You're made
out of gold and-a

can't be sold. ___   So-er,   are you ex-per-i - enced?   Ah! have you ev-er been ex -

per-i-enced? ___   Well, ___   I   have. ___   Ah, let me prove it to you.

Trum-pets and vi-o- lins   I can   hear in the dis-tance.   I think they're call-ing our   names.

___   May-be now ___ you can't hear them,   but you will ___   if you

just   take hold of my hand. ___   Ah! ___ but   are you ex - per-i - enced?

Have you ev -er   been ex- per-i - enced?   Not necessarily stoned,   but beautiful.

Manic Depression
Words and music by Jimi Hendrix

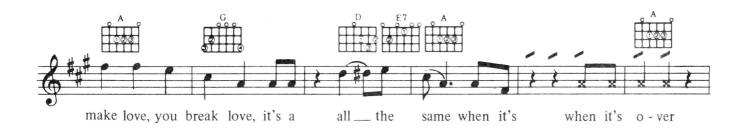

make love, you break love, it's a   all __ the   same when it's   when it's o - ver

Mus - ic sweet mus - ic,   I wish   I could ca - ress   ca - ress   ca-ress. _

To Coda ⊕

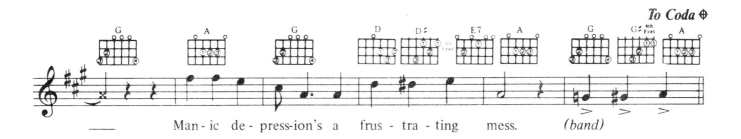

____ Man - ic de - press-ion's a   frus - tra - ting   mess.   *(band)*

Well I   think I'll go   turn my-self off an'   go on down.

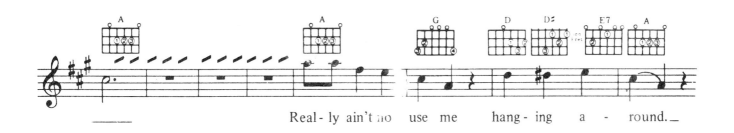

_____ Real - ly ain't no   use me   hang - ing   a - round. _

D. S. al Coda

Oh I   got - ta see you.

⊕ *CODA*

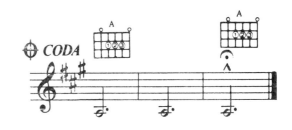

Gypsy Eyes
Words & music by Jimi Hendrix

Moderately

no chords

Well, I re - al - ize ___ that I've been hyp - no - tized; ___ I love you

Gyp - sy Eyes, _____   I love you Gyp - sy Eyes. _____

Way up

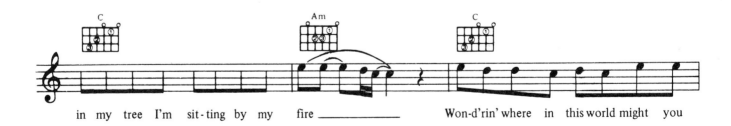

in my tree I'm sit - ting by my fire _____   Won-d'rin' where in this world might you

be. ___ And know-ing all are roam-in' the coun-try-side. ___

no chords

Do you still think a - bout me? (Oh, my) (Gypsy Eyes)

ADDITIONAL WORDS

Well, I walk right on up to your rebel roadside
The one that rambles on for a million miles
Well, I walk down this road
Searching for your love and-uh my soul too
And when I find you, I ain't gonna let go.

I remember the first time I saw you
The tears in your eyes look like they was try'n' to say
"Oh, little boy, you know I could love you
But first, I must make my getaway,
Two strange men fighting to the death over me today . . . . .
I'll try to meet you by the old highway. '

Well, I realize that I've been hypnotized
I love you, Gypsy Eyes . . . . I love you, Gypsy Eyes
I love you, Gypsy Eyes . . . . I love you, Gypsy Eyes.

I've been searching so long,
My feet, they painfully leave the battle
Down against the road my weary knees take their place
Off to the side I fall
But I hear a sweet call
My Gypsy Eyes has found me and I've been saved
Lord, I've been saved
That's why I love you
Lord knows, I love you.

Voodoo Chile
Words and music by Jimi Hendrix

Moderately fast Blues

no chords

Well, I stand up next to a moun-tain   And I chop it down

with the edge of my hand. ___

Well, I stand up next to a moun-tain _____

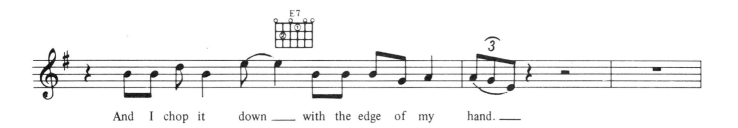

And I chop it down _____ with the edge of my hand. _____

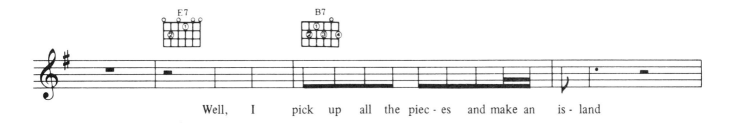

Well, I pick up all the piec-es and make an is-land

might e-ven raise just a lit-tle sand.

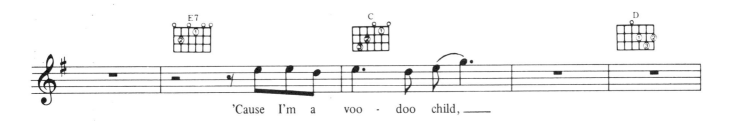

'Cause I'm a voo-doo child, _____

Lord, knows, I'm a voo-doo child, ba-by.

ADDITIONAL WORDS

I didn't mean to take up all your sweet time
I'll give it right back to you one of these days.
I didn't mean to take up all your sweet time
I'll give it right back one of these days.
And if I don't meet you no more in this world;
Then I'll meet you in the next one, so don't be late, don't be late.
'Cause I'm a voodoo child (voodoo child) Lord knows, I'm a voodoo child.

Da Ya Think I'm Sexy?

Words and music by Rod Stewart and Carmine Appice

CHORUS

Dm7 ... you want my bo - dy and ... you think I'm sex - y come ... on, sug-ar let me know. ... If ...

Dm7 ... you real-ly need me just ... reach out and touch me, come ... on hon - ey tell me so. ...

(2) He's act - ing shy look-ing for an ans - wer come on ... hon-ey, ... let's

spend the night to - ge - ther, ... now hold on ... a "min" be - fore we go much fur-ther,

give me a dime ... so I can 'phone my moth-er. They catch a cab to his

high rise a - part-ment, at last he can tell her ex - act - ly what his heart meant. If ...

___ you want my bod - y and __ you think I'm sex - y come __ on, hon - ey tell me so. ___ If ___

sug - ar let me know.

Instrumental section

__ you real - ly need me just __ reach out and touch me, come __ on sug-ar let me know. __

hon - ey, tell me so. _____

His

heart's beat - ing like a drum __ 'cos at last he's got this girl home.

___ Re - lax ba - by now we're all a - lone. __ *D.%.*

(Repeat instrumental section
ad lib. till fade)

Verse 3: They wake at dawn 'cos all the birds are singing,
Two total strangers but that ain't what they're thinking.
Outside it's cold misty and it's raining,
They got each other neither one's complaining,
He says I'm sorry but I'm out of milk and coffee,
Never mind sugar, we can watch the early movie.

Hot Legs
Words and music by Rod Stewart

Moderate Rock Beat

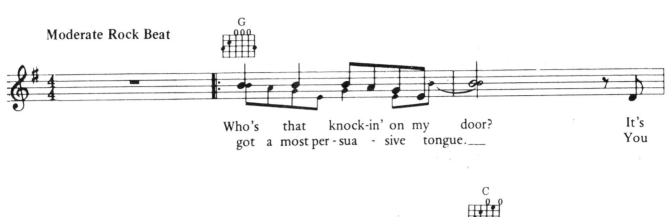

Who's that knock-in' on my door? It's
got a most per-sua-sive tongue.___ You

got-ta be a quar-ter to four.___ Is it you___ a-gain,___
prom-ise all kinds of fun.___ But what you don't un-der-stand,__

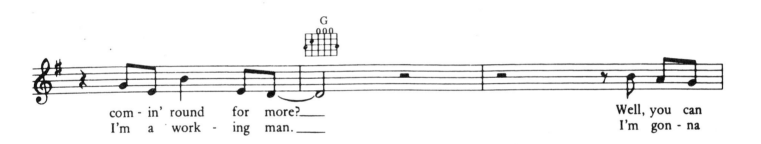

com-in' round for more?___ Well, you can
I'm a work-ing man.___ I'm gon-na

love me to-night___ if you want,_____ but in the
need a shot of vi-ta-min E_____ by the

morn-ing make sure you're gone.___ I'm talk-in' to you:
time you're fin-ished with me.___ I'm talk-in' to you:

Hot legs, you're wear-in' me out.___ Hot legs, you can
Hot legs, you're an al - ley cat.___ Hot legs, you

scream and shout.___ Hot legs, are you still in school?___
scratch my back.___ Hot legs, bring your moth-er too.___

I love you, hon - ey. You
I love you, hon - ey. I -

mag - ine how my dad - dy felt, ___ in your jet - black sus-pend-er belt.___

___ Sev-en - teen years old, ___ he's trudg-ing six - ty-four. ___

You got legs right up to your neck.___ You're mak-in'

me a   phys - i - cal   wreck. ___   I'm   talk - in'   to   you:

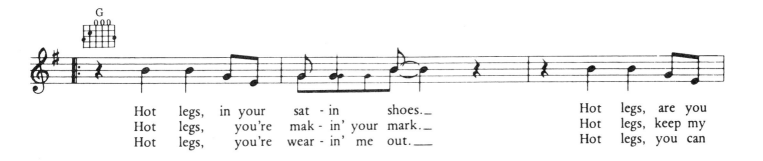

Hot   legs,   in your   sat - in   shoes. _   Hot   legs,   are you
Hot   legs,   you're   mak - in' your mark. _   Hot   legs,   keep my
Hot   legs,   you're   wear - in' me   out. ___   Hot   legs,   you can

still   in   school? _   Hot legs, you're mak - in' me   a   fool. _
pen - cil   sharp. _   Hot legs,   keep your   hands to your-self. _
scream and   shout. _   Hot legs,   you're   still   in   school. _

1. 2. | 3.
Tacet   N.C.   Tacet   N.C.

I love you, hon-ey.   I love you, hon-ey.
I love you, hon-ey.

Hot   legs.   Hot   legs.

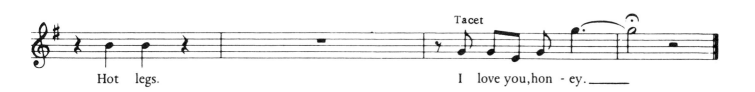

Hot   legs.   I love you, hon - ey. _____

Tonight's The Night
Words and music by Rod Stewart

Moderately slow Rock beat

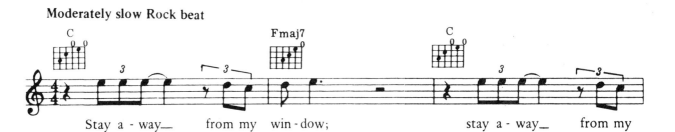

Stay a - way___ from my win - dow; stay a - way___ from my

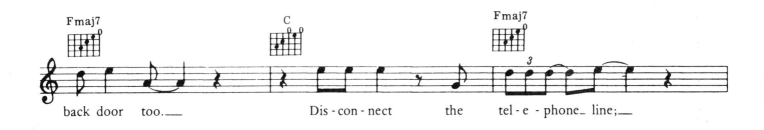

back door too.___ Dis - con - nect the tel - e - phone_ line;___

re - lax, ba - by, and draw that blind.___

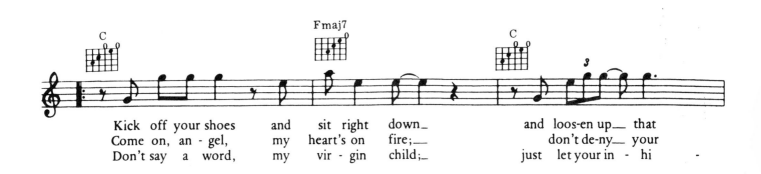

Kick off your shoes and sit right down_ and loos-en up__ that
Come on, an - gel, my heart's on fire;___ don't de-ny__ your
Don't say a word, my vir - gin child;__ just let your in - hi -

pret-ty French gown.

Let me pour you a good long drink;

man's de - sire.

You'd be a fool to stop this tide;

bi-tions run wild.

The se - cret is a - bout to un - fold

ooh, ba - by, don't you hes - i - tate. } 'Cause

spread your wings and let me come in - side. }

up - stairs be - fore the night's too old. }

to - night's the night; it's gon-na be al -

right. 'Cause I love you, girl; ain't no

bod - y gon - na stop us now.

95

Is That The Thanks I Get

Words and music by Rod Stewart and Jim Cregan

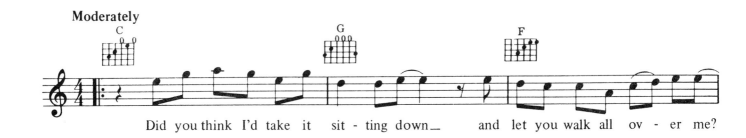

Did you think I'd take it sit-ting down __ and let you walk all ov-er me?

Thought you knew me much bet - ter than that, __ I

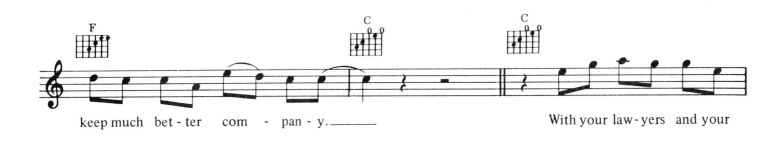

keep much bet-ter com-pan-y. __ With your law-yers and your

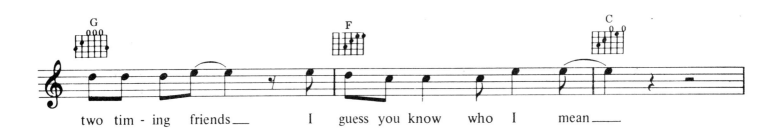

two tim-ing friends __ I guess you know who I mean __

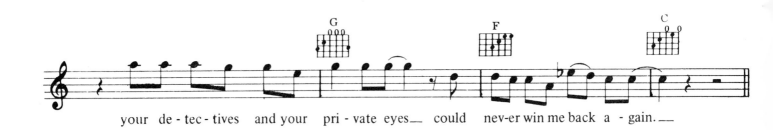

your de-tec-tives and your pri-vate eyes __ could nev-er win me back a-gain. __

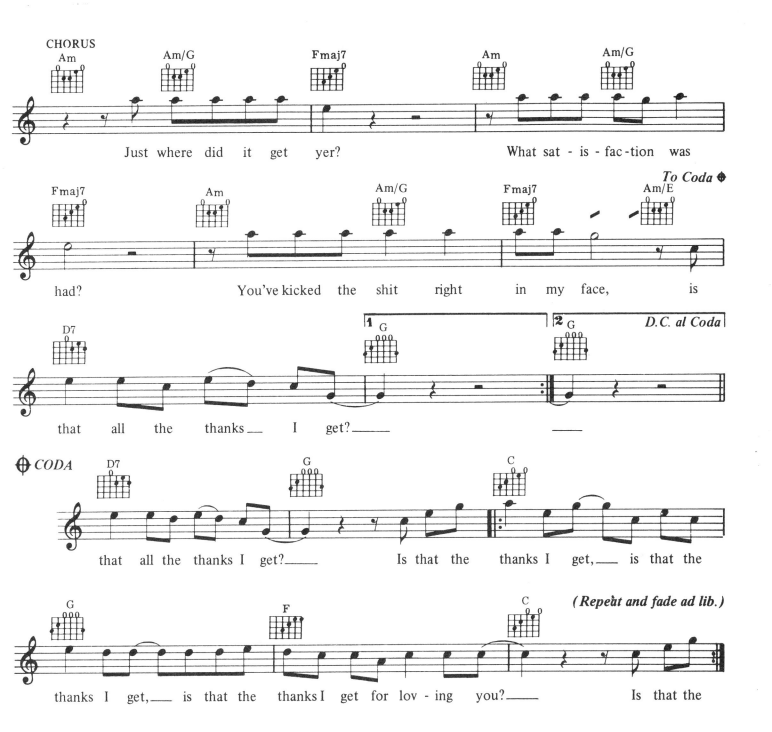

Verse 2: You said we made a pretty pair, living in harmony,
I'm sorry honey but I disagree, it seemed more like a comedy.

Chorus: Just look how you lied girl, that Judas right by your side,
He hung you up so you cut me right down, is that the thanks I get.

Verse 3: Guess I'll find me a brand new girl, that won't take too very long,
There's so many floatin' 'round this town, waitin' by the telephone.
And if you want me I'll be in the bar back into my usual ways
Or on the corner with the rest of the boys, you and I were just a breath away.

Chorus: It was great while it lasted, but oh Lord it turned nasty,
You didn't give me one chance to explain, is that all the thanks I get.
Is that the thanks I get, is that the thanks I get, is that the
Thanks I get for loving you?

(Repeat last two lines for fade)

97

Ain't Love A Bitch
Words and music by Rod Stewart and Gary Grainger

she took — me way up - stairs — and she wiped me clean

Oh I — did -n't re - al - ize — she made a first class fool out of me. —

1 2 *(2nd time to *)*

Oh Mag - gie if you're still out there — the rest is his - to - ry.

3 D.C. al Coda

⊕ CODA

smile. (4) Tor -

(Spoken ad lib.) Ain't love a bitch.

Repeat and fade ad lib.

Verse 2: You're all alone in the freezin' cold, by the underground,
Your hands are numb and you're feelin' dumb 'cos you bin let down,
You thought you were rough and kinda tough and maybe out of reach, you're
Acting chic playing hide 'n' seek, but ain't love a bitch.

Chorus (2): Oh I must state right here I've been there before. My eyes
were closed, and so my friends I still don't know the score.
Oh don't underestimate the strength of it, it may be unwise,
To analyse even the cause of it.

½ Verse 3: You're drivin' home late one night, and on the radio
(from *) Comes an old familiar song you used to know so well (you know a lot about that).

Chorus (3): Oh I can't comprehend this thing called love,
Maybe it's a matter of fact I just can't grow up.
Deep down, ain't we all a little juvenile (just a boy),
All I really wanna know, is there one sweet angel that
Can make me smile.

Verse 4: Torrential rains, wars and hurricanes I wouldn't budge an inch.
But your rent's unpaid and yer team lose again but
Ain't love a bitch,
You can lose your job, your home and your head,
But ain't love a bitch.
Take it or leave it, some day you'll feel it 'cos
Love is the bitch.

To Coda

Sailing

Words and music by Gavin Sutherland

Slow beat

I am

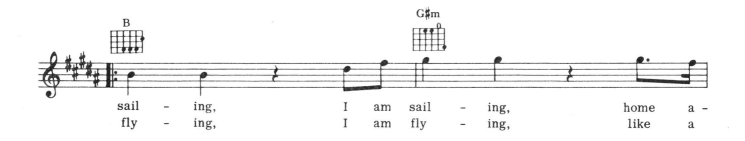

sail - ing,   I am sail - ing,   home a -
fly - ing,   I am fly - ing,   like a

gain _   'cross the sea.   I am sail - ing   stor - my
bird _   'cross the sky.   I am fly - ing   pass - ing

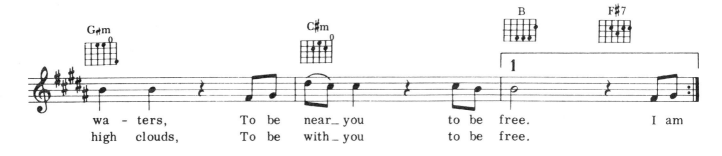

wa - ters,   To be near _ you   to be free.   I am
high clouds,   To be with _ you   to be free.

free   Can you hear me,   Can you hear me,   Thro' the

Tusk
Words and music by Lindsey Buckingham

Moderately

Why don't_ you ask him if he's gon - na stay? ___
Why don't_ you tell me what's go - in' on? ___

Why don't_ you ask him if he's go - in' a - way? ___
Why don't_ you tell me who's on __ the phone? ___

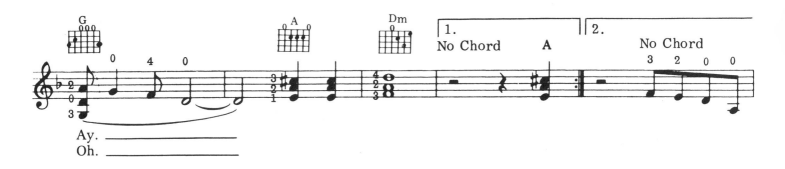

Ay. ___
Oh. ___

1. No Chord   A   2. No Chord

Why don't_ you ask him what's go - in' on? _ Why don't_ you ask him the

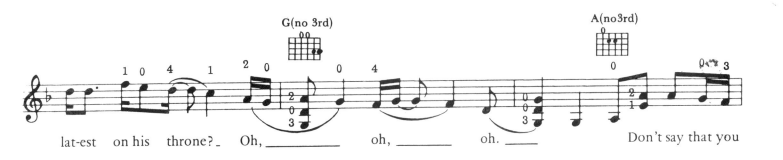

lat-est on his throne?_ Oh, _____ oh, _____ oh. ____ Don't say that you

love me.

Just tell me that you want me.

Tusk! Just say that you want me.

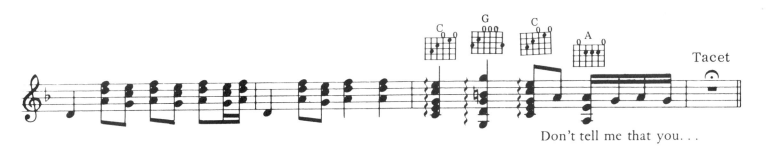

Don't tell me that you. . .

Repeat and fade

Tusk!

Don't Stop

Words and music by Christine McVie

1. If you wake up and don't want to smile; ___ if it takes just a lit - tle while, o - pen your eyes and look at the day. ___ You'll see things in a dif - f'rent ___ way. ___

Chorus

Don't stop think - ing a - bout to - mor - row. Don't stop.

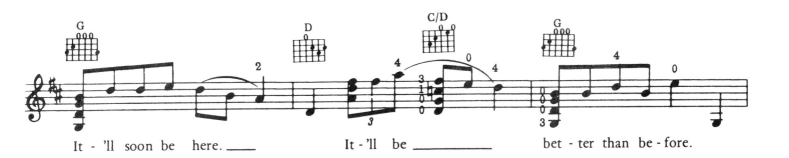

It - 'll soon be here. _____ It - 'll be _____ bet - ter than be - fore.

Yes - ter - day's gone. _ Yes - ter - day's gone. _____ Yes - ter - day's gone. _____

Repeat and fade

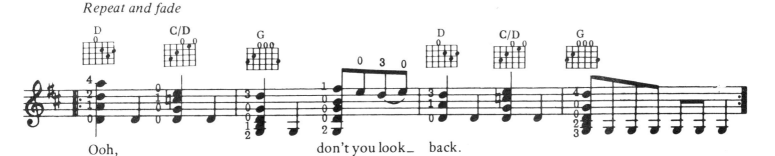

Ooh, don't you look_ back.

Additional lyrics

2. Why not think about times to come,
   And not about the things that you've done.
   If your life was bad to you,
   Just think what tomorrow will do.

   Chorus

3. All I want is to see you smile,
   If it takes just a little while.
   I know you don't believe that it's true.
   I never meant any harm to you.

   Chorus

Rhiannon
Words and music by Stevie Nicks

Moderately bright

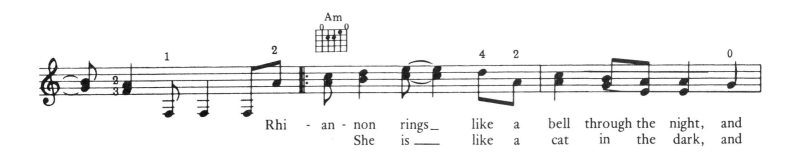

Rhi - an - non rings＿ like a bell through the night, and
She is ＿ like a cat in the dark, and

would-n't you love ＿ to love ＿ her?
then she is ＿ the dark - ness.

Takes to the sky like a
She rules her life like a

bird in flight,＿ and who will be ＿ her lov - er?
fine sky - lark ＿ and when the sky＿ is star - less.

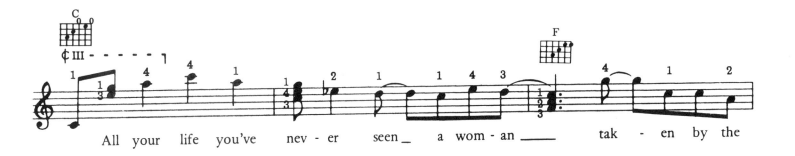

All your life you've nev - er seen __ a wom - an __ tak - en by the

wind. __ Would you stay if she prom - ised you heav - en?

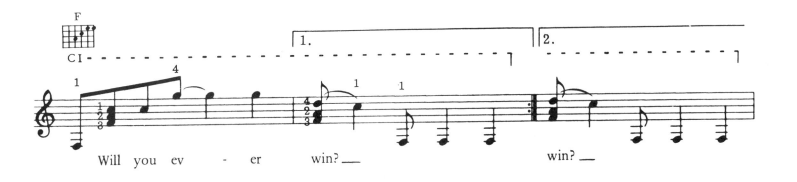

Will you ev - er win? __ win? __

Repeat and fade

Will you ev - er win? __ Dreams un - wind. Love's __

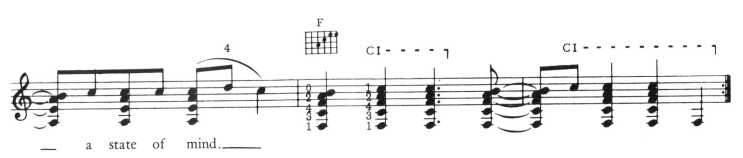

__ a state of mind. __

Songbird
Words and music by Christine McVie

Moderately and gently

1. For ____ you, ____ there'll be no more

cry - in'. For ____ you, _____

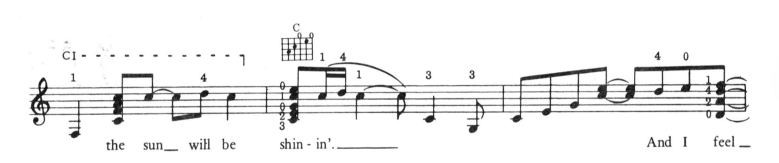

the sun__ will be shin - in'._____ And I feel __

__ that when_ I'm with__ you, it's al - right. _____ I know it's

right.__ 2. To

And the song - birds _____ are sing - ing like they know the score. _

And I love_ you, I love_ you, I love_

_ you like nev - er be - fore. _____

But most of all, _ I _____ wish it from_ my - self. _

And the song - birds _____ keep sing -

ing like they know the score. _____ And I love_

_ you, I love_ you, I love _ you like nev - er be - fore. _____

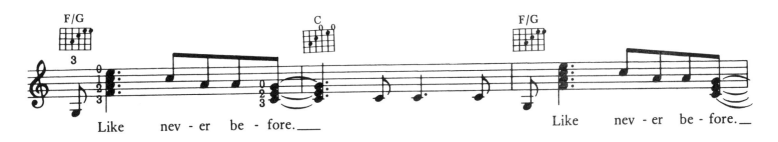

Like nev - er be - fore.___   Like nev - er be - fore._

_____   *rit.*

Additional lyrics

2. To you, I'll give the world.
   To you, I'll never be cold.
   'Cause I feel that when I'm with you, it's alright.
   I know it's right.
   And the songbirds are singing *(etc.)*

3. *Instrumental* _____

   And I wish you all the love in the world.
   But most of all, I wish it from myself.
   And the songbirds keep singing *(etc.)*

Carry On
Words and music by Stephen Stills

Medium beat

1. One morn - ing I woke up and I knew you were

real - ly gone. A new day,

a new way, and new eyes to see the dawn.

Go your way, I'll go mine

and car - ry on.

row.____ Are they ques - tions of ___ a thou - sand dreams?_

What you do___ and what___ you see._ Lov - er can__ you talk_

____ to me?_____

Repeat and fade

Additional lyrics part $\boxed{A}$

2. The sky is clearing and the night has cried enough,
   The sun it comes, the world to soften up.
   Rejoice, rejoice, we have no choice but to carry on.

3. The fortunes of fables are able to see the stars,
   Now witness the quickness with which we carry on.
   To sing the blues, you've got to live the dues and carry on.

Additional lyrics part $\boxed{B}$

Girl, when I was on my own, chasing you down,
What was it made you run? Tryin' your best just to get around.
The questions of a thousand dreams: What you do and what you see.
Love, can you talk to me?

113

At Seventeen
Words and music by Janis Ian

1. I learned the truth at sev - en - teen_ that love was meant for beau -
2. (A) brown-eyed girl in hand - me - downs_ whose name I nev - er could_
3. (To) those of us who know_ the pain_ of val - en - tines that nev -

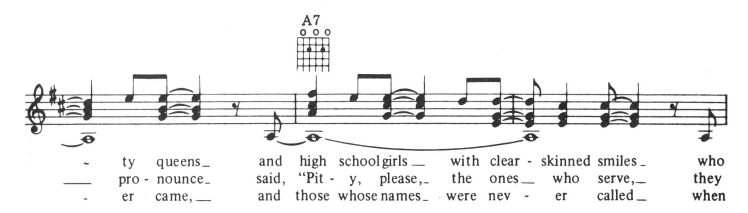

- ty queens_ and high school girls _ with clear - skinned smiles_ who
____ pro - nounce_ said, "Pit - y, please, the ones_ who serve,_ they
- er came, __ and those whose names_ were nev - er called_ when

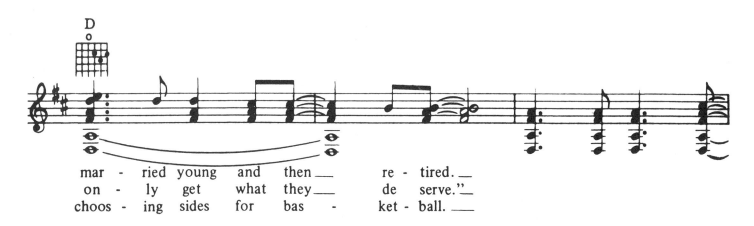

mar - ried young and then _ re - tired. _
on - ly get what they _ de serve."
choos - ing sides for bas - ket - ball. __

The val - en - tines I nev - er knew,_ the
The rich re - la - tioned home - town queen_ ____
It was long a - go and far __ a - way. __ The

Fri - day night cha - rades _ of youth _ were spent on one _ more beau -
mar - ries in - to what _ she needs _ A guar - an - tee _ of com -
world was young - er than _ to - day _ and dreams were all _ they gave _

- ti - ful _ At sev - en - teen, I learned _ the truth. _
- pa - ny _ And ha - ven for the el - der - ly. _
_ for free _ to ug - ly duck - ling girls _ like me. _

And those of us _ with rav -
Re - mem - ber those _ who win _
We all play the game _ and when _

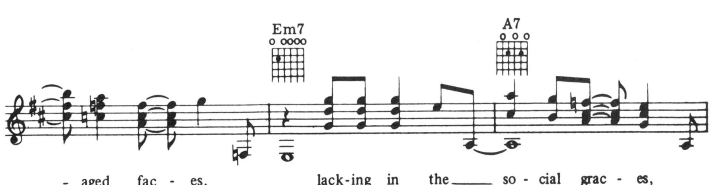

- aged fac - es, lack - ing in the _ so - cial grac - es,
_ the game _ lose the love they _ sought to gain _ In
_ we dare _ to cheat our - selves at _ sol - i - taire _ In -

Des - p'rate-ly ___ re - mained ___ at home ___ in - vent - ing lov - ers on ___
de - ben - tures ___ of qual - i - ty ___ and du - bi - ous in - teg -
vent - ing lov - ers on ___ the phone, ___ re - pent - ing oth - er lives ___

___ the phone ___ Who called to say, ___ "Come dance ___ with me," ___ and
- ri - ty. ___ Their small town eyes ___ will gape ___ at you ___ in
___ un - known ___ that call and say, ___ "Come dance ___ with me," ___ and

mur - mured vague ___ ob - scen - i - ties. ___ It is - n't all it
dull sur - prise ___ when pay - ment due ___ ex - ceeds ac - counts re -
mur - mur vague ___ ob - scen - i - ties. ___ at ug - ly girls like

1.& 2.

seems   at sev - en - teen.   2. A
ceived   at sev - en - teen.   3. To
me   at sev - en - teen.

3.

116

Riki Tiki Tavi

Words and music by Donovan

Bright beat

Bet-ter get in - to   what you got___ to get in - to

bet-ter get in - to it   now no slack-ing   please___

u - nit - ed___ na - tions___ ain't real-ly u - nit - ed   and the

or-gan-i - za - tions ain't_ real-ly or - gan-ized _____

Ri -ki - ti - ki ta - vi mon - goose_ is gone

Ri -ki -ti - ki ta - vi mon - goose_ is gone won't be

com-in' a round_ for to kill your snakes no more_ my love (Guitar)

Ri -ki ti -ki ta - vi mon - goose_ has gone (Guitar) ev- 'ry

-bod- y who read_ the jun-gle book a-knows that Ri-ki ti-ki ta-vi's a mon-goose who kills

snakes   well when I was a young man I was led to be-lieve there were organizations to

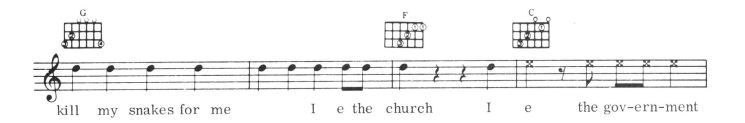

kill   my snakes for me   I   e the church   I   e   the gov-ern-ment

I   e   the school   but when I got a lit-tle old – er   I

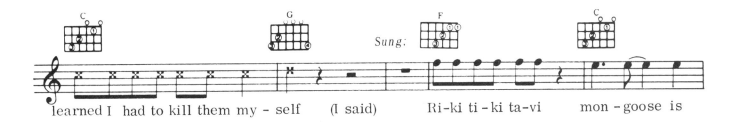

learned I had to kill them my - self   (I said)   Ri-ki ti -ki ta-vi   mon - goose is

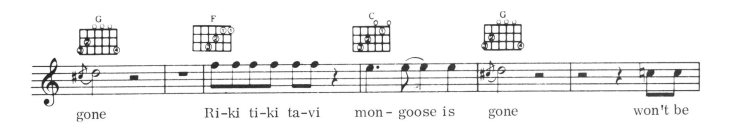

gone   Ri-ki ti-ki ta-vi   mon - goose is   gone   won't be

com-in' a - round for   to   kill your snakes   no   more— my love

119

(Instrumental)

Ri - ki ti - ki ta - vi mon- goose— is gone

(Guitar fill in)

3 times

Peo-ple walking around they

don't know what they're do - in' they bin lost so long they don't—

— know what they're look-ing for —— Well I

know what I'm a-look-in' for —— but I just can't find it I

120

guess I got-ta look in - side of my - self_ some more _____

(Bass) oh   oh   oh   In - side o' my-self_ some   more_

_ (come on now)   Ri -ki ti -ki ta -vi   mon - goose_ is   gone

I   saw you to - day_____   on a num - ber twelve_

bus you were go - ing my   way _____

(Instrumental)

my   way

121

Don't It Make My Brown Eyes Blue
Words and music by Richard Leigh

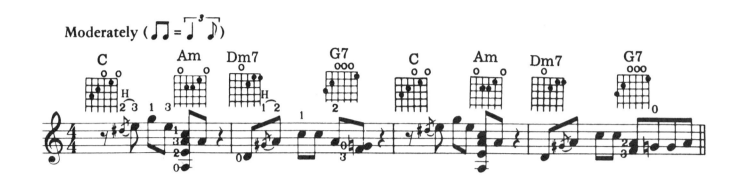

1. Don't know when   I've been so blue, _____   don't know what's come
2. I'll be fine   when you're gone, _____   I'll just cry
3. I did-n't mean   to treat you bad, _____   did-n't know just

o - ver you, _____   you've found some-one new _____   and
all night long, _____ say it is - n't true _____   and
what I had, _____   but hon - ey now I do _____   and

Don't It Make My Brown Eyes   Blue. _____   Don't It Make My Brown Eyes

Blue.   Tell me no se - crets.   tell me some lies,

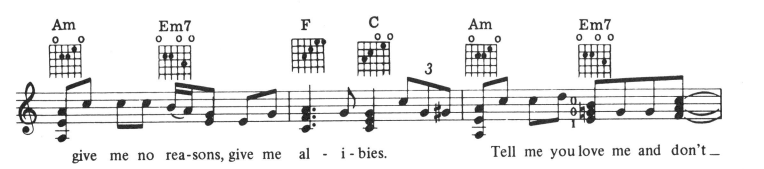

give me no rea-sons, give me al - i - bies.   Tell me you love me and don't __

D. S. al Coda

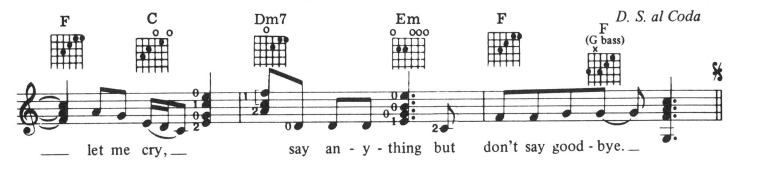

__ let me cry, __   say an - y - thing but don't say good - bye. __

Repeat and fade

Coda

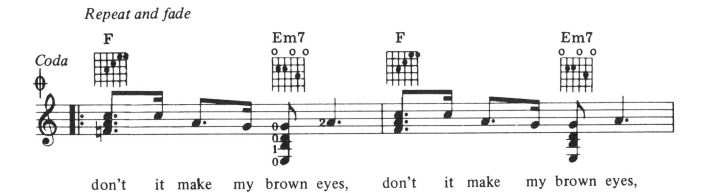

don't   it make my brown eyes,   don't   it make   my brown eyes,

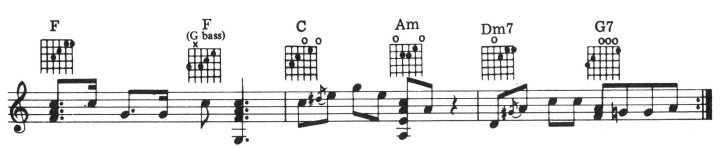

Don't It Make My Brown Eyes   Blue.

Stoned Soul Picnic
Words and music by Laura Nyro

Can you sur - rey, ___ can you pic - nic? Wo _____ Can you

sur - rey, ___ can you pic - nic?

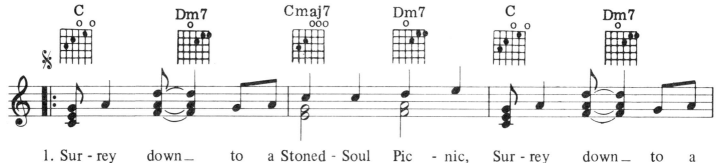

1. Sur - rey down_ to a Stoned - Soul Pic - nic, Sur - rey down_ to a
2. Sur - rey down_ to a Stoned - Soul Pic - nic, Sur - rey down_ to a
3. Sur - rey down_ to a Stoned - Soul Pic - nic, Sur - rey down_ to a

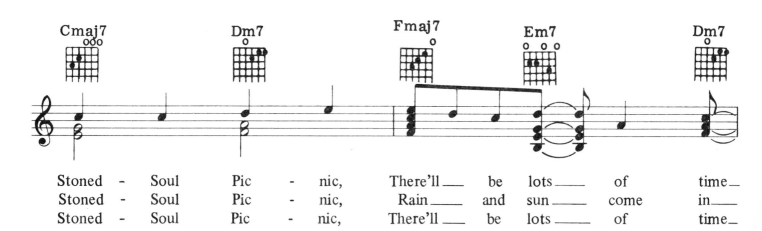

Stoned - Soul Pic - nic, There'll_ be lots_ of time_
Stoned - Soul Pic - nic, Rain__ and sun __ come in_
Stoned - Soul Pic - nic, There'll_ be lots_ of time_

and wine. ___ Red, yel - low hon - ey,
a - kin. ___ And from the sky come the
and wine. ___ Red, yel - low hon - ey,

Sas - sa - frass and moon - shine. Red, yel - low hon - ey, Sas -
Lord and the light - nin'. And from the sky come the
Sas - sa - frass and moon - shine. Red, yel - low hon - ey, Sas -

sa - frass and moon - shine. ___ ⎫
Lord and the light - nin'. ___ ⎬ Stoned - soul, ___
sa - frass and moon - shine. ___ ⎭

___ stoned - soul. ___

2.

___ Sur - ry on soul. Sur - ry, ___

125

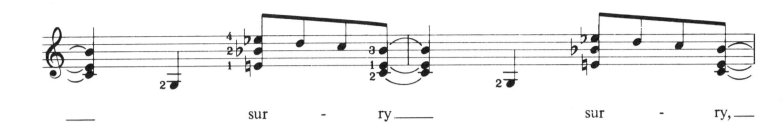

sur - ry _____ sur - ry, _____

sur - ry, _____ There'll be

trains of blos - soms, _____ There'll be

trains of mu - sic. (There'll be mu - sic.) There'll be

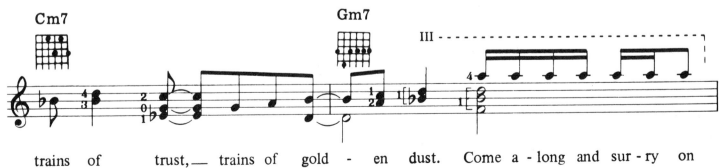

trains of trust,_ trains of gold - en dust. Come a - long and sur - ry on

sweet trains _____ of thought sur-ry on down.

Can you sur - ry? Can you sur - ry? _____

Moon - shine, stoned - soul.

Yeah! _____ Sur-ry on soul.

Repeat and fade

Sur - ry sur - ry.

Cold As Ice

Words and music by Mick Jones and Lou Gramm

Short People
Words and music by Randy Newman

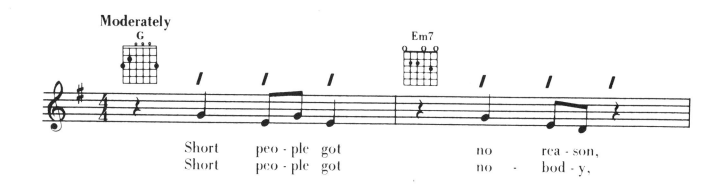

Short peo - ple got no rea - son,
Short peo - ple got no - bod - y,

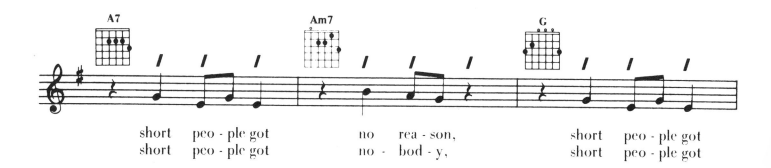

short peo - ple got no rea - son, short peo - ple got
short peo - ple got no - bod - y, short peo - ple got

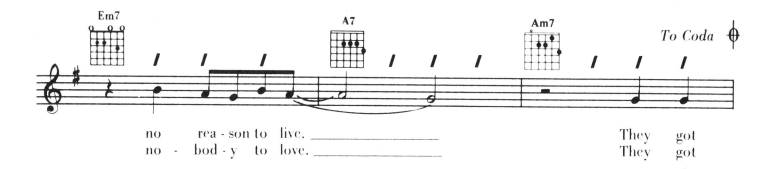

no rea - son to live. _____ They got
no - bod - y to love. _____ They got

lit - tle hands. __ lit - tle eyes, __ they walk a-round tell-in'

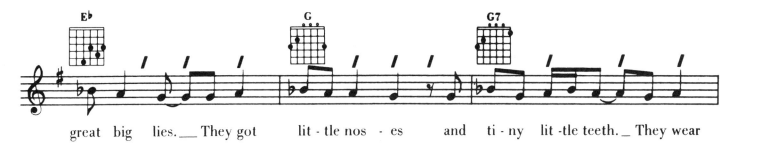

great big lies. __ They got lit - tle nos - es and ti - ny lit -tle teeth. _ They wear

plat - form shoes on their nas - ty lit-tle feet. __ Well, I don't want no

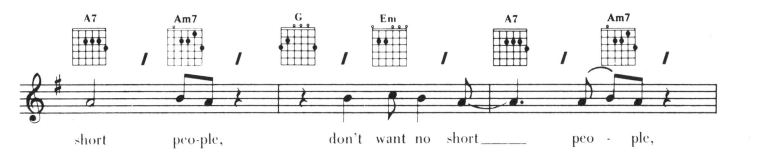

short peo-ple, don't want no short_____ peo - ple,

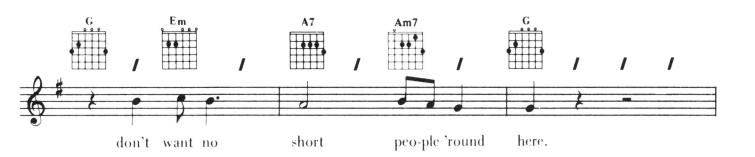

don't want no short peo-ple 'round here.

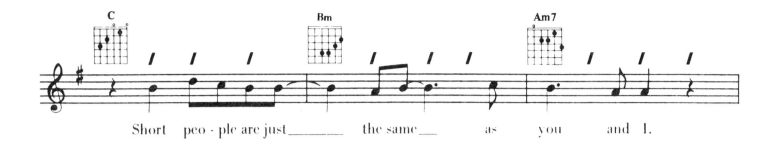

Short peo - ple are just_____ the same___ as you and I.

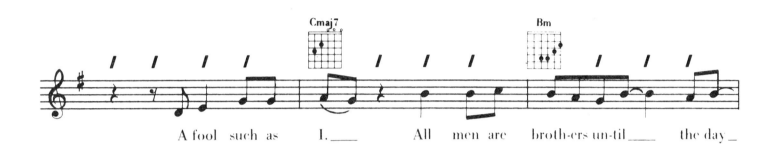

A fool such as I.___ All men are broth-ers un-til___ the day_

___ they die.____ It's a won - der - ful world

lit - tle ba - by legs they stand so low. You got to pick 'em up ___ just to

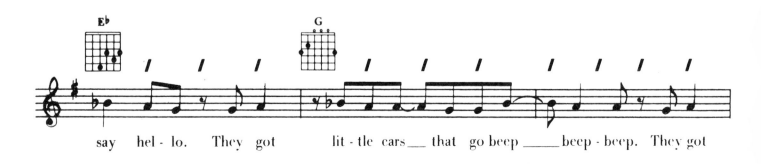

say hel - lo. They got lit - tle cars___ that go beep ____ beep - beep. They got

lit - tle voic - es go - in' peep-peep - peep. They got grub-by lit - tle fin-gers and

dirt- y lit - tle minds; _ they're gon-na get you ev - 'ry time. __ Well, I

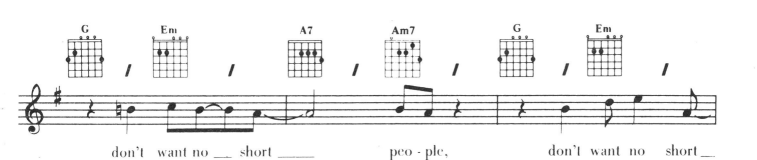

don't want no __ short _____ peo - ple, don't want no short __

_____ peo - ple, don't want no short peo-ple 'round

here.
(sing 1st time only)

Mr. Blue Sky
Words and music by Jeff Lynne

Sun is shin - in' in the sky,— there ain't— a cloud in sight.—
(2nd instr.)

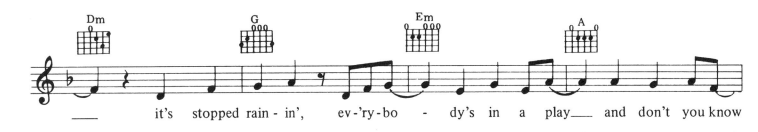

— it's stopped rain - in', ev - 'ry - bo - dy's in a play— and don't you know

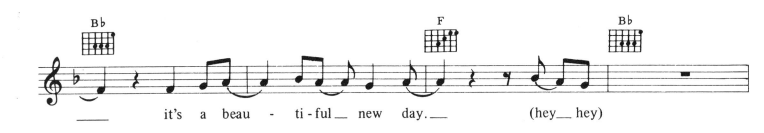

— it's a beau - ti - ful— new day.— (hey— hey)

(1) Run - nin' down the av - en - ue,— see how the sun shines
(2) Hey you with the pret - ty face,— wel - come to the hu - man

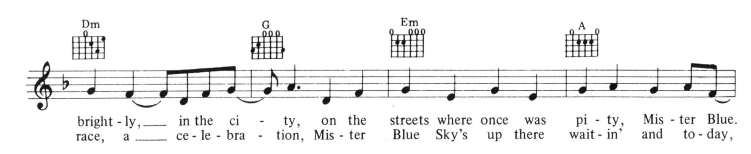

bright - ly,— in the ci - ty, on the streets where once was pi - ty, Mis - ter Blue.
race, a — ce - le - bra - tion, Mis - ter Blue Sky's up there wait - in' and to - day,

Sky is liv-ing here to day, ___ (hey___ hey)
___ is the day we've wait-ed for, ___ (ah___ ah)

Mis-ter Blue Sky___ please tell us why___ you had to hide ___ a-way_ for

so long; where did we go wrong? Mis-ter Blue Sky___

___ please tell us why___ you had to hide___ a-way___ for so long;

where did we go wrong?

Hey there, Mis-ter Blue, ___ we're so pleased to

be with you, ___ look a-round, see what you do, ___ ev-'ry-bo-dy

135

smiles at you.___ Hey there Mis - ter Blue,___ we're so pleased to

be with you,___ look a - round, see what you do___ ev - 'ry - bo - dy

smiles at you.___ Mis - ter Blue Sky,

Mis - ter Blue Sky

Mis - ter Blue Sky._____

Mis -ter Blue___ you did it right___ but soon comes Mis - ter Night,___ creep - ing ov -

- er, now his hand___ is on___ your shoul - der, ne - ver mind,___ I'll re-mem-

Turn To Stone
Words and music by Jeff Lynne

The ci - ty streets_ are emp - ty now___ (The lights don't shine___
The dy - ing emb - ers of __ the night. __ (A fire that slow -
The danc - ing shad - ows on __ the wall ___ (The two - step in __

___ no more ___) and so__ the songs_ are way_ down low ___ (turn-ing
- ly fades till dawn) still glow up-on __ the wall_ so bright__ (burn-ing,
___ the hall ___) are all __ I see__ since you've been gone __ (turn-ing,

turn-ing, turn-ing) A sound that flows_ in - to __ my mind,__ (The ech-oes of __
burn-ing, burn-ing) The ti - red streets that hide__ a - way ___ (From here to ev -
turn-ing, turn-ing) Through all__ I sit __ here and __ I wait ___ (I turn to stone_

___ the day - light ___) of ev - 'ry - thing __ that is ___ a - live_
- 'ry - where they go ___) roll past __ my door __ in - to __ the day_
___ I turn __ to stone ___) you will __ re - turn __ a - gain __ some day_

___ (in my blue world -))
___ (in my blue world -))   I turn to stone when
___ (in my blue world -))

you are gone, I turn___ to stone. Turn to stone, when you com-

-in' home, I can't__ go on.

Turn to stone, when you are gone, I turn___ to stone. Yes I'm

turnin' to stone 'cause you ain't comin' home, Why ain't you comin' home if I'm turnin' to stone, You've been

gone for so long and I can't car-ry on, Yes I'm turn-in', I'm turn-in' I'm turn-in' to stone.

D.C. al Coda   ⊕ *CODA*

turn to stone when you are gone, I turn

To FADE

___ to stone.

Telephone Line
Words and music by Jeff Lynne

feel - in'?   Are you   still   the   same,— don't you re - a - lize — the

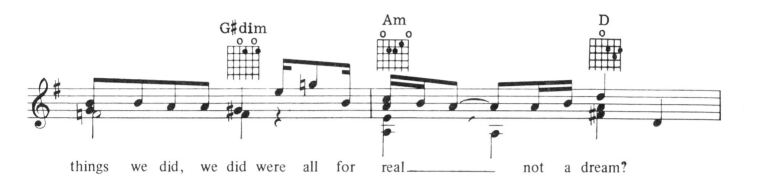

things   we did,   we did were all   for   real_____ not   a dream?

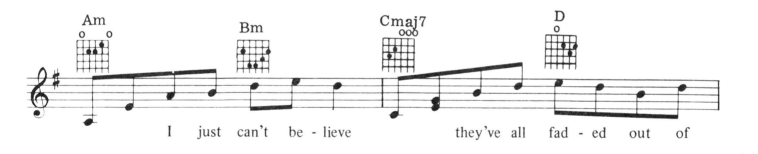

I   just   can't   be - lieve   they've   all   fad - ed   out   of

view,   yeah, yeah, yeah, yeah,_____   oo._____

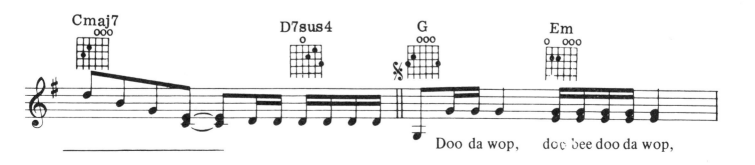

_____   Doo da wop,   doo bee doo da wop,

doo wah doo lang._____ Blue days, black nights,___

doo wah doo lang._____ I look in - to the sky,

The love you need ain't gon - na see you through,___

And I won-der why the lit-tle things you planned ain't com - in' true.___

Fade (after 3rd verse)

Oh, oh, Tel - e - phone Line,___ Give me some time,___

___ I'm liv - ing in twi light.

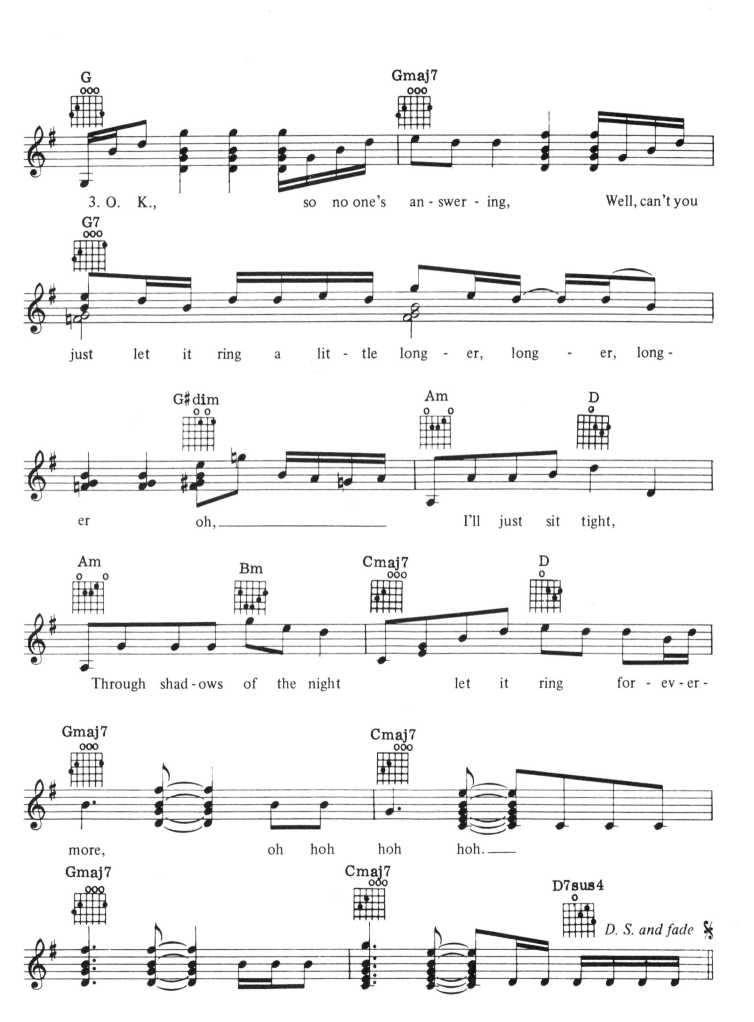

3. O. K., so no one's an-swer-ing, Well, can't you

just let it ring a lit-tle long-er, long - er, long-

er oh,_____ I'll just sit tight,

Through shad-ows of the night let it ring for-ev-er-

more, oh hoh hoh hoh.____

D. S. and fade

Shine A Little Love
Words and music by Jeff Lynne

Al-though the things you've done   I   would-n't cri-tic-ise
mem-ber to-night___ we're gon-na   run   'till   dawn,   re-

mem-ber   to-night we're gon-na   say it._
I guess you had your   way. _   You see, I've got-ta make you
We'll nev-er stop, we got a

un-der-stand,_   I know it sounds a fool-ish   thing to say._   But it
good thing go-in' on   I know you heard it   all be-fore,_   and I

don't mat-ter ba-by, 'cause to-day's an-oth-er day.
real-ly need you darl-in', ev-'ry day I need you more.   You shine a lit-tle love on my life_

you shine a lit-tle love on my life. ____

You shine a lit-tle love on my life_____ and let me see.

144

Re -

Can you un - der - stand?,_ yes I un - der - stand._ Can you

feel it's right?_ I know it is.__ Will you be the same?_ I'll do it

all a - gain. __ Oo oo oo wa oo wa

oo wa oo wa oo!

{ It's been a year now and it's
{ how man - y days had I been

get - ting so much bet - ter,   you came home with - out a word._
wait - ing there to tell you,   I real - ly can't be - lieve__

Though ev - 'ry -bo- dy said, "You'll soon for-get ____ her." They could-n't see and they just
we're walk-ing out in - to the world to -night. We'll do it all a -gain un -

did- n't un-der- stand, and the look-in' in the mir - ror, there were fools at ei -ther hand.
til the break of light, and the feel - in' in your heart will soon be

shin - ing in your eyes. You shine a lit -tle love on my life, ___

you shine a lit -tle love on my life, ____

you shine a lit -tle love on my life ____ and let me see.

to FADE

146

Before The Deluge
Words and music by Jackson Browne

Moderately

1. Some of them were dream-ers__ and some of them__ were

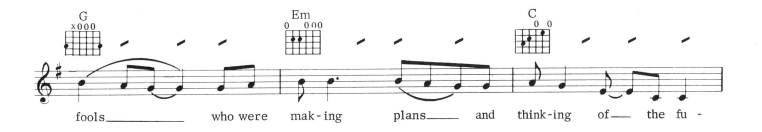

fools_____ who were mak-ing plans__ and think-ing of __ the fu -

ture. With the en - er - gy__ of the in - no - cent, they were

gath - er - ing the tools_____ they would need to make their__

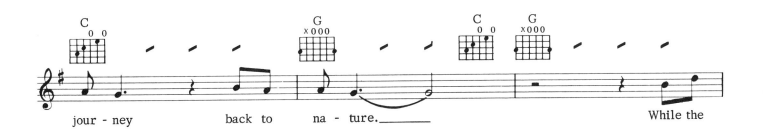

jour - ney back to na - ture._____ While the

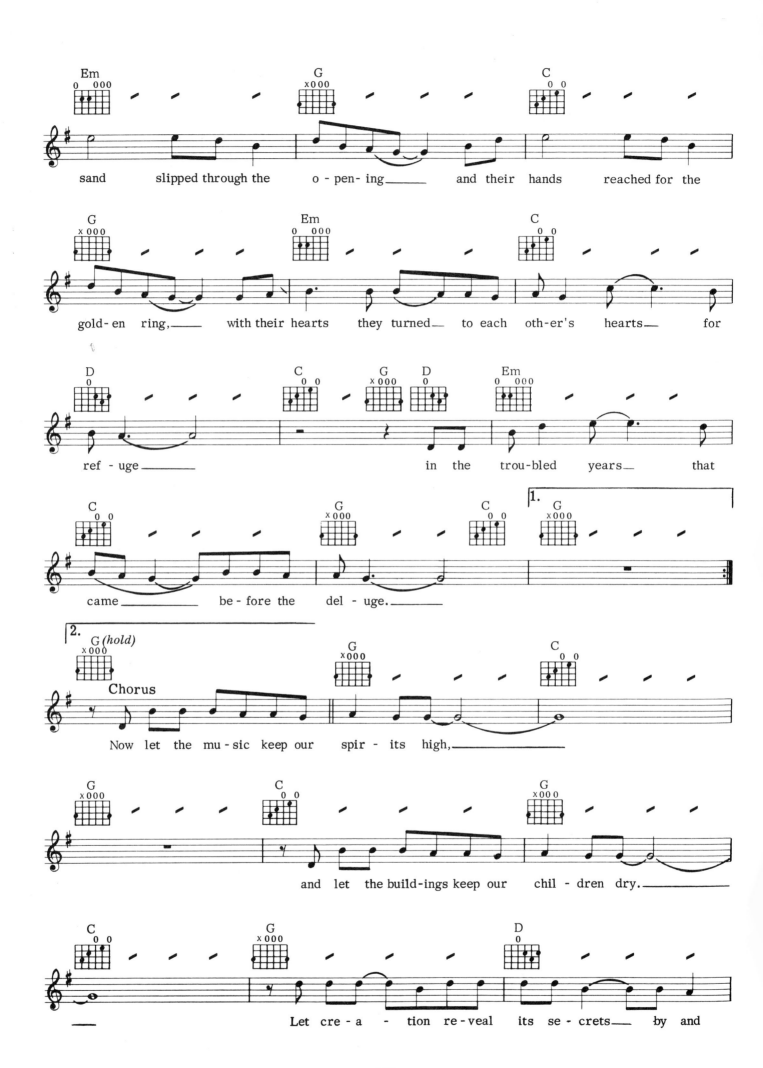

sand _____ slipped through the o - pen- ing_____ and their hands reached for the
gold-en ring,_____ with their hearts they turned___ to each oth-er's hearts___ for
ref - uge _____ in the trou-bled years___ that
came _____ be - fore the del - uge._____

Chorus
Now let the mu - sic keep our spir - its high,_____
and let the build-ings keep our chil - dren dry._____
_____ Let cre - a - tion re-veal its se - crets_____ by and

2. Some of them knew pleasure and some of them knew pain,
   And for some of them it was only the moment that mattered.
   On the brave and crazy wings of youth they went flying around in the rain,
   And their feathers, once so fine, grew torn and tattered.
   And in the end they traded their tired wings
   For the resignation that living brings,
   And exchanged love's bright and fragile glow
   For the glitter and the rouge,
   And in a moment they were swept before the deluge.

(Chorus)

3. Some of them were angry at the way the earth was abused
   By the men who learned how to forge her beauty into power.
   And they struggled to protect her from them only to be confused
   By the magnitude of her fury in the final hour.
   And when the sand was gone and the time arrived
   In the naked dawn only a few survived,
   And in attempts to understand a thing so simple and so huge,
   Believed that they were meant to live after the deluge.

(Chorus)

Redneck Friend
Words and music by Jackson Browne

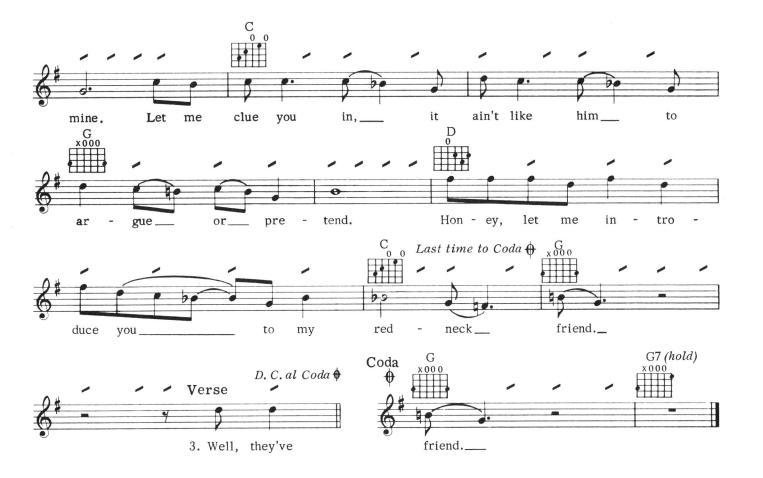

mine. Let me clue you in, ___ it ain't like him ___ to ar - gue ___ or ___ pre - tend. Hon - ey, let me in - tro - duce you ___ to my red - neck ___ friend. ___

Last time to Coda

D. C. al Coda Verse

3. Well, they've

Coda friend. ___

Verse 2. Now your daddy's in the den shootin' up the evening news;
Mama's with a friend, lately she's been so confused.
Little one, come on and take my hand.
I may not have the answer but I believe I got a plan.

Chorus I. Honey, you shake and I'll rattle and we'll roll on down the line, *(etc.)*

Verse 3. Well, they've got a little list of all those things of which they don't approve;
They've got to keep their eyes on you or you might make your move.
Little one, I really wish you would.
Little one, I think the damage would do you good.

Chorus II. Honey, you shake and I'll rattle and we'll roll on down the line.
We're going to forget all about the battle; it's gonna feel so fine.
'Cause he's the missing link, the kitchen sink, eleven on a scale of ten.
Honey, let me introduce you to my redneck friend.

Chorus III. Honey, you shake and I'll rattle and we'll roll on down the line.
I'm going to try to swing you up into my saddle, and then we'll run but you'll think we're flyin'.
Now, honey, don't just stand there lookin' like this dream will never end.
Honey, let me introduce you to my redneck friend.

Listen To The Music
Words and music by Tom Johnston

oh, _____ lis-ten to the mu - sic.__ Oh, __

oh, _____ lis-ten to the mu - sic.__ Oh, __

oh, _____ lis-ten to the mu - sic__ all the

time. _____

Like a la - zy flow - ing riv - er _____ sur -round -ing

cas - tles in the sky. _____ And the

crowd is grow - ing big - ger, _____ lis - t'nin' for the

D. S. and fade

hap - py sounds,_ and I got to let__ them fly. Oh, ___

Natural Thing
Words and Music by Tom Johnston

Good Times, Bad Times
Words and Music by Mick Jagger and Keith Richards

Moderate

There've been good   times   There've been bad

times.   I've had   my   share___   of   hard times___   too.___

___   But   I   lost   my___   faith in the world_____

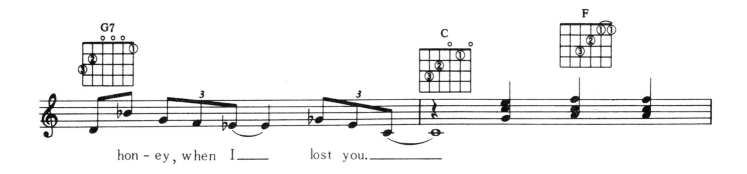

hon - ey, when I____ lost you.____

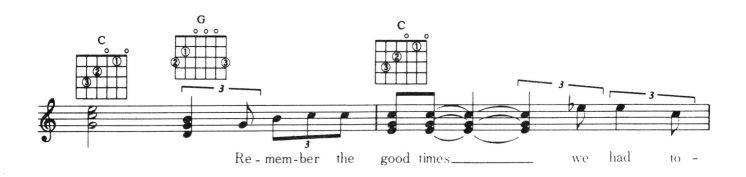

Re - mem - ber the good times_____ we had to -

geth - er ?___ Don't you want them_ back a - gain ?___ Tho' these

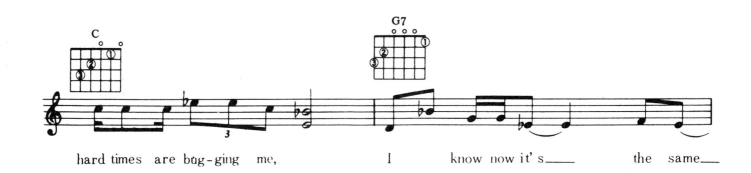

hard times are bug - ging me, I know now it's____ the same____

There's got-to-be trust in this world,

or it won't get ver-y far. Well,

trust-ing someone, or just gon - na be war,

(Hum) etc.

(This Could Be) The Last Time
Words and Music by Mick Jagger and Keith Richards

Moderate

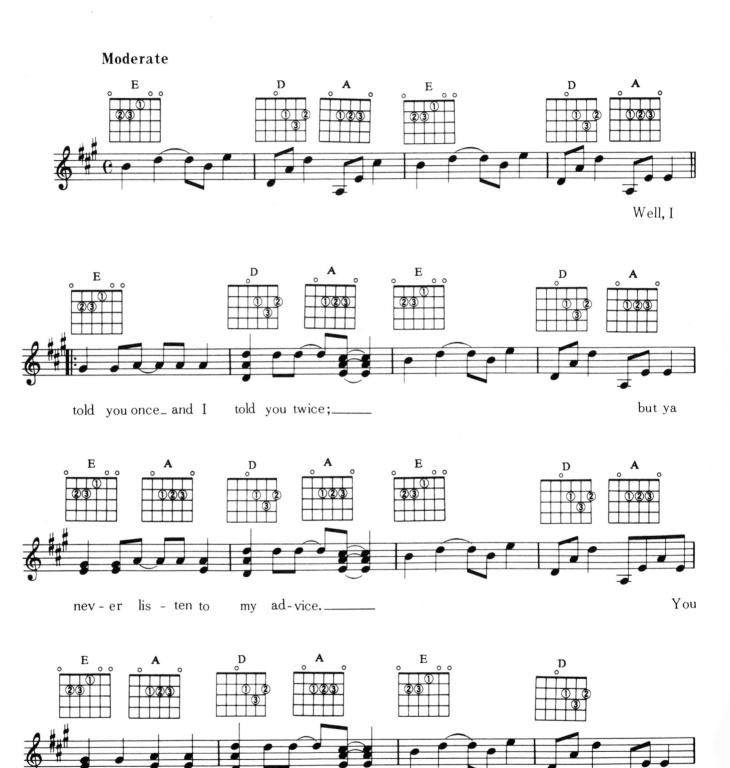

Well, I told you once_ and I told you twice;_____ but ya

nev-er lis-ten to my ad-vice._____ You

don't try ver-y hard to please_ me;__ with

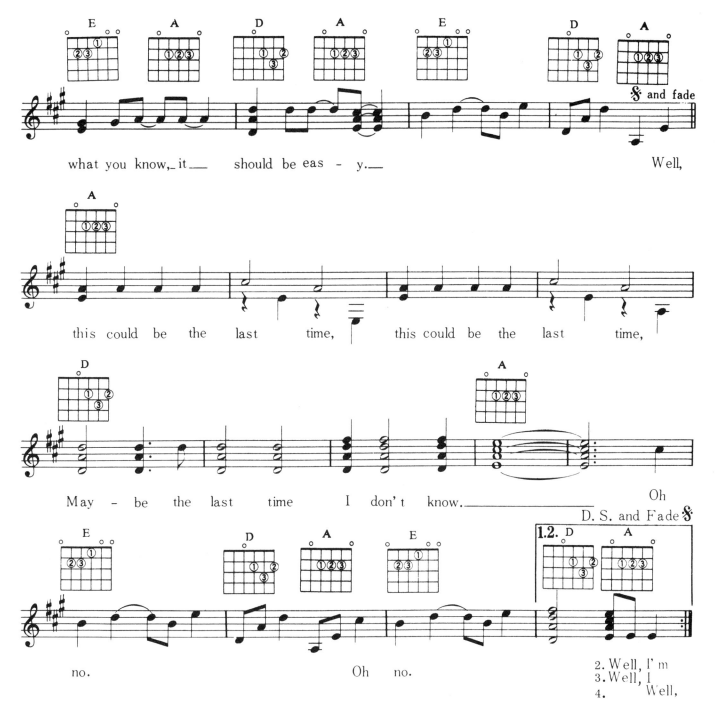

what you know,_ it _ should be eas - y._ Well,

this could be the last time, this could be the last time,

May - be the last time I don't know._ Oh

no. Oh no.

2. Well, I'm
3. Well, I
4. Well,

2. Well, I'm sorry girl but I can't stay
feelin' like I do today.
It's too much pain and too much sorrow;
guess I'll feel the same fomorrow.

3. Well, I told you once and I told you twice;
that someone else will have to pay the price.
But here's a chance to change your mind
'cuz I'll be gone a long, long time.

159

Let's Spend The Night Together

Words and Music by Mick Jagger and Keith Richards

Moderate

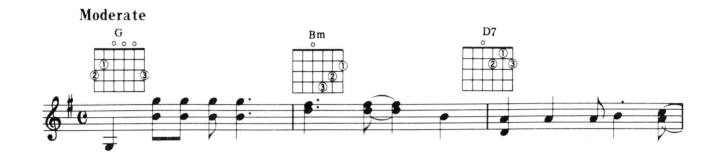

Don't you wor-ry 'bout what's on your mind.__ (Oh my.)
I feel so strong that I can't dis - guise,__ (Oh my.)

I'm in no hur-ry, I can
But I just can't a -

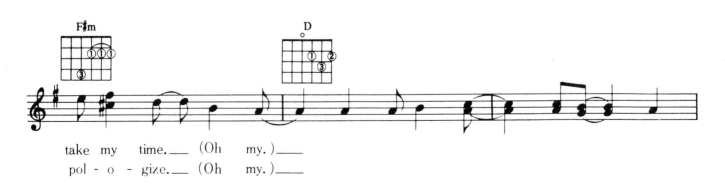

take my time.__ (Oh my.)___
pol - o - gize.__ (Oh my.)___

160

I'm go - ing red_____ and my tongue's__ get - ting tied,___
Don't hang me up_____ and don't_____ let me down.__

____ I'm off my head__
____ We could have fun__

____ and my mouth's get - ting dry._____ I'm high,___ But I
____ just groov - in' a - round._____

try, try, try,__ (Oh, my.)___ } Let's Spend The Night__ To - geth - er.

Now I need you more___ than ev - er, Let's Spend The Night_

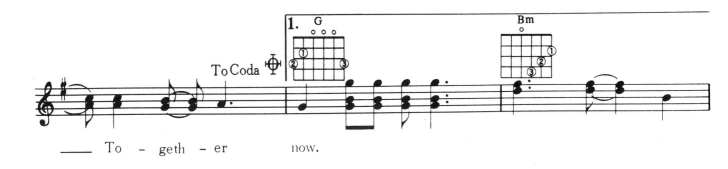

To Coda

To - geth - er now.

Let's Spend The Night

To - geth - er, Now I need you more than ev - er.

You know I'm smil - ing ba - by.

You need some guid - ing, ba - by, I'm just de - cid -

162

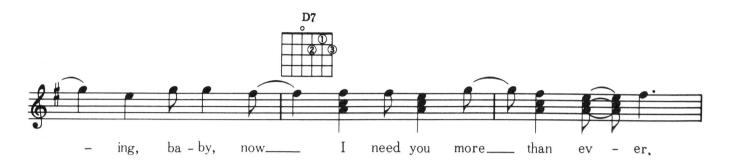

– ing, ba - by, now____ I need you more____ than ev – er.

Let's Spend The Night____ To - geth – er,   Let's Spend The Night _

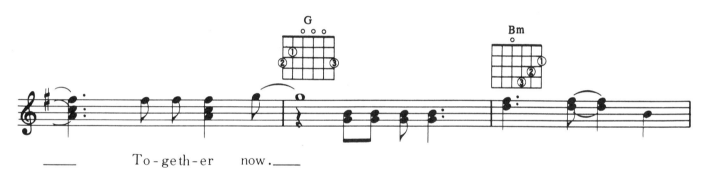

____ To - geth - er now.____

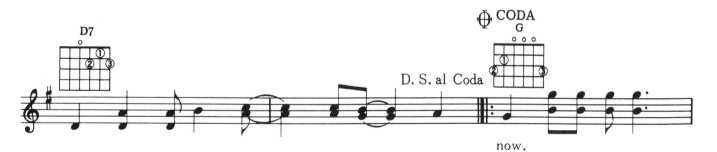

D. S. al Coda   CODA

now.

Let's Spend The· Night ____ To - geth – er.

Mother's Little Helper

Words and music by Mick Jagger and Keith Richards

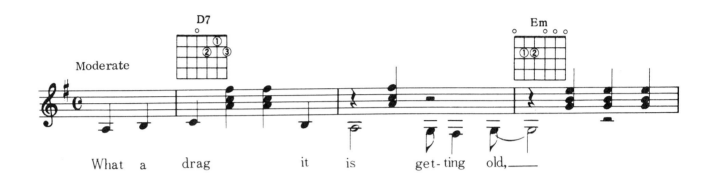

What a drag   it is   get-ting old,___

"Kids are dif-fer-ent___ to-day,"___   I hear ev'-ry moth-er   say.___

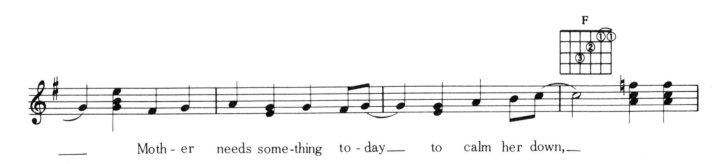

___ Moth-er   needs some-thing to-day___ to   calm her down,___

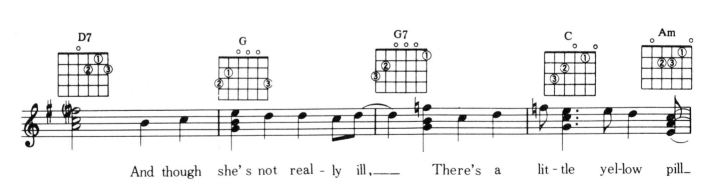

And though   she's not real-ly ill,___   There's a   lit-tle   yel-low   pill___

She goes run-ning for the shel-ter of a moth-er's lit-tle

help - er, And it helps her on her way.__ Gets her through__ her bus-y day.

Last time to ⊕ Coda 𝟏.

𝟐.𝟑.

"Things are

Doc-tor please__

Some more these.__

Out - side the door,

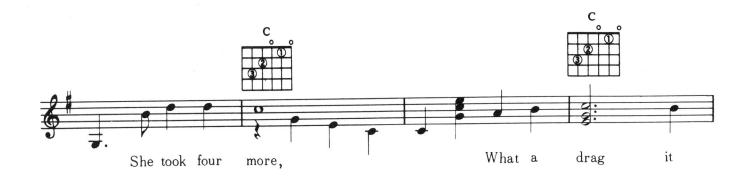

She took four more, What a drag it

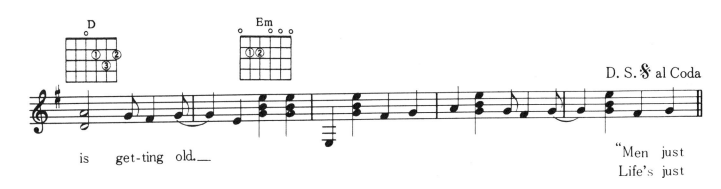

D. S. 𝄋 al Coda

is get-ting old. —

"Men just
Life's just

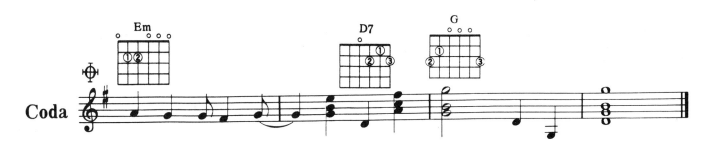

Coda

2. "Things are different today",
   I hear ev'ry mother say,
   Cooking fresh food for a husband's just a drag.
   So she buys an instant cake and she burns her frozen steak
   And goes running to the shelter of a mother's little helper
   And two help her on her way, get her through her busy day.

3. "Men just aren't the same today,"
   I hear ev'ry mother say,
   They just don't appreciate that you get tired.
   They're so hard to satisfy, You can tranquilize your mind
   So go running to the shelter of a mother's little helper
   And four help you through the night, help you minimize your plight.

4. "Life's just much too hard today,"
   I hear ev'ry mother say,
   The pursuit of happiness just seems a bore
   And if you take more of those, you will get an overdose.
   No more running to the shelter of a mother's little helper
   They just helped you on your way through your busy dying day,

Have You Seen Your Mother Baby

Words and Music by Mick Jagger and Keith Richards

Moderately Fast

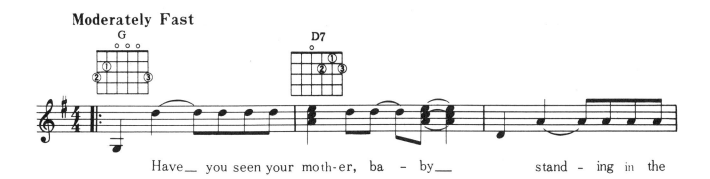

Have_ you seen your moth-er, ba - by_ stand - ing in the

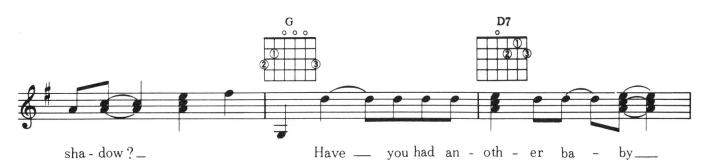

sha - dow?_ Have _ you had an - oth - er ba - by_

stan - ding in the sha - dow?_ I'm glad I

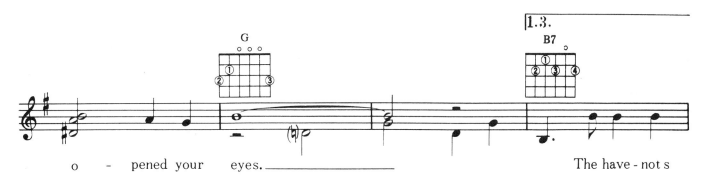

o - pened your eyes._____ The have - nots

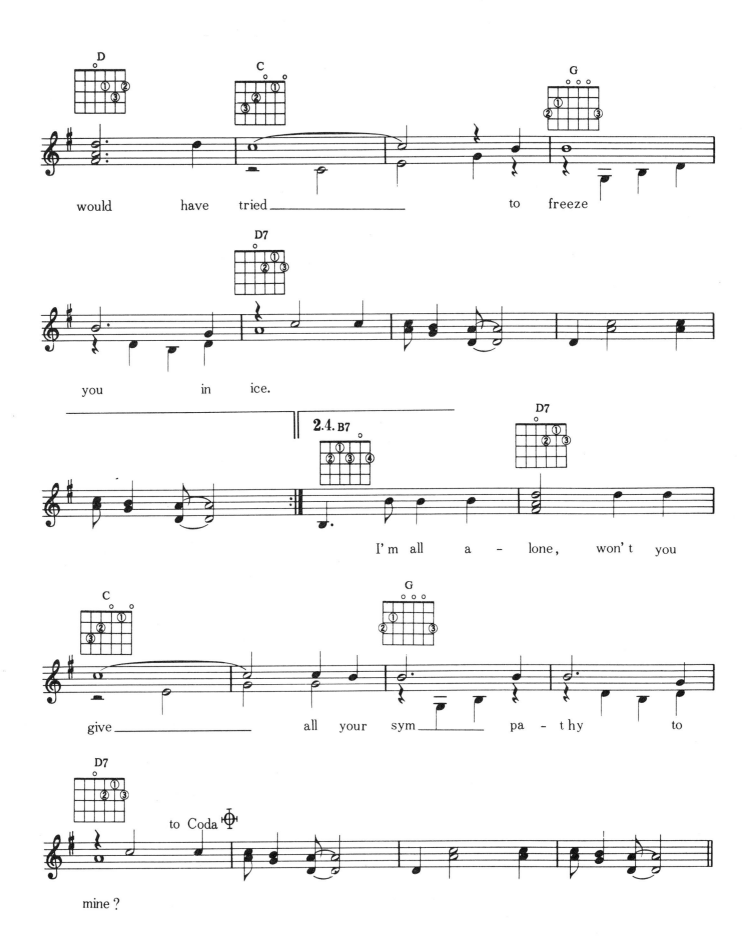

would have tried _____ to freeze

you in ice.

2.4. B7

I'm all a - lone, won't you

give _____ all your sym____ pa - thy to

to Coda

mine ?

Tell_____ me a sto - ry___ a-bout how_____ you a -
Live_____ in the sha - dow,___ how we see_____ through the
Glimpse___ through the sha - dow,___ how we tear_____ at the
Hate _____ in the sha - dow, how we live_____ in your

dore me,___ how we sha - dow ___ y life.
sha dow,___ how we
sha dow,___ how we

D. S. 𝄋 al 𝄌 Coda

Coda

2. Have you seen your brother, baby standing in the shadow?
   Have you seen another baby standing in the shadow?
   I was just passing the time.

3. Have you seen your lover, baby standing in the shadow?
   Has he had another baby standing in the shadow?
   Where have you been all your life?

4. Have you seen your mother, baby standing in the shadow?
   Have you had another baby standing in the shadow?
   You take your choice at this time.

19th Nervous Breakdown

Words and Music by Mick Jagger and Keith Richards

Moderately Bright

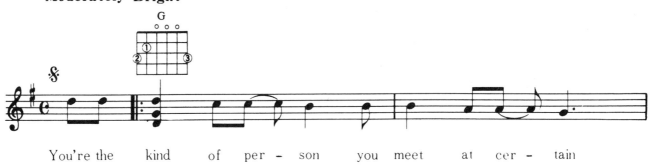

You're the kind of per - son you meet at cer - tain

dis - mal, dull af - fairs. _ Cen-ter of a crowd, _ talk - ing

much too loud, _ run-ning up and down the stairs. _ Well, it

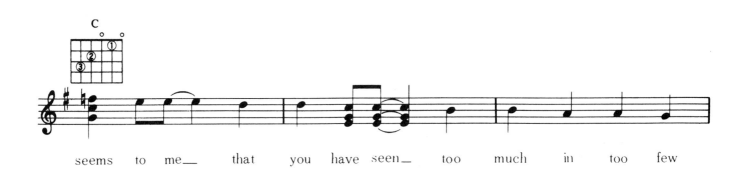

seems to me _ that you have seen _ too much in too few

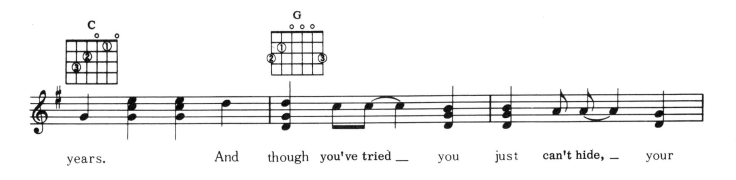

years.   And   though **you've tried** __   you   just   **can't hide,** __   your

eyes   are edged with tears, __   You bet-ter stop,

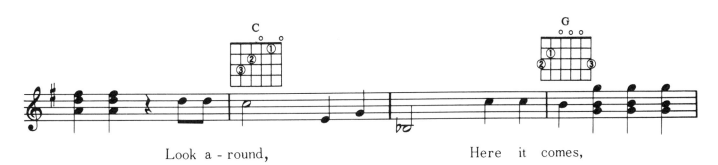

Look a - round,   Here it comes,

here   it   comes,   here   it

comes, ___   Here it comes.

to Coda

Here comes your Nine - teenth Ner - vous Break - down.

1. G

— When you

2. G

Oh, who's to

blame, that girl's just in -

sane. Well, noth - in' I do don't

172

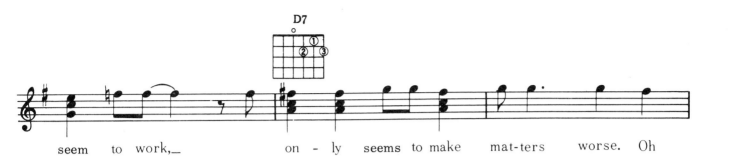

seem to work,__ on - ly seems to make mat-ters worse. Oh

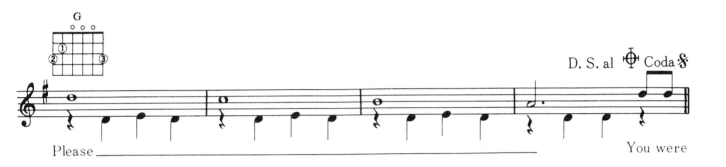

D. S. al ⊕ Coda 𝄋

Please _____ You were

Coda

comes your Nine-teenth Ner-vous Break - down.__ Here

2. When you were a child you were treated kind
   But you were never brought up right.
   You were always spoiled with a thousand toys but still you cried all night.
   Your mother who neglected you owes a million dollars tax.
   And your father's still perfecting ways of making ceiling wax.

3. You were still in school when you had that fool who really messed your mind.
   And after that you turned your back on treating people kind.
   On our first trip I tried so hard to rearrange your mind.
   But after while I realized you were disarranging mine.

Play With Fire

Words and music by Mick Jagger/Keith Richards/Bill Wyman/Charlie Watts/Brian Jones

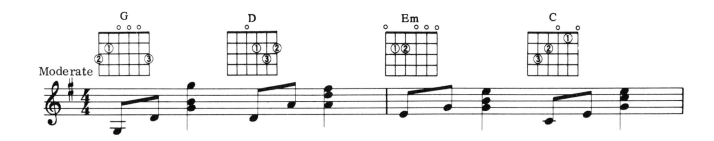

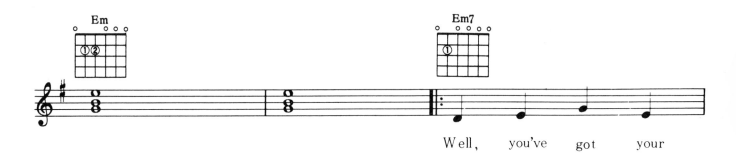

Well, you've got your

dia - monds and you've got your pret - ty clothes, And the

chau - ffeur drives your car.___ You let ev' - ry - bod - y

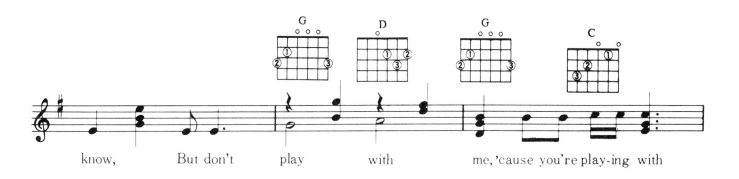

know, But don't play with me, 'cause you're play-ing with

fire.   2. Your fire.
                                                         4. Your

2. Your old man took her diamonds and tiaras by the score.
   Now she gets her kicks in Stepney, not in Knightbridge anymore;
   So don't play with me, 'cause you're playing with fire.

3. Now you've got some diamonds and you will have some others;
   But you'd better watch your step, girl,
   Or start living with your mother;
   So don't play with me, 'cause you're playing with fire.

175

Street Fighting Man
Words and Music by Mick Jagger and Keith Richards

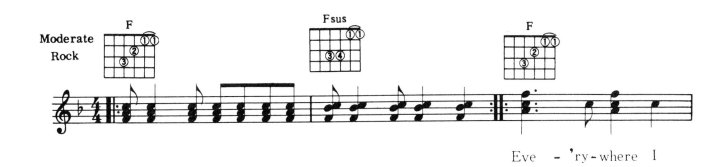

Eve – 'ry-where I

hear the sound of march-ing, charg-ing feet, Oh, Boy. 'Cause

sum - mer's here and the time is right for fight-ing in the street, Oh,

Boy. But what can a poor boy do ex-cept to sing for a Rock 'N' Roll

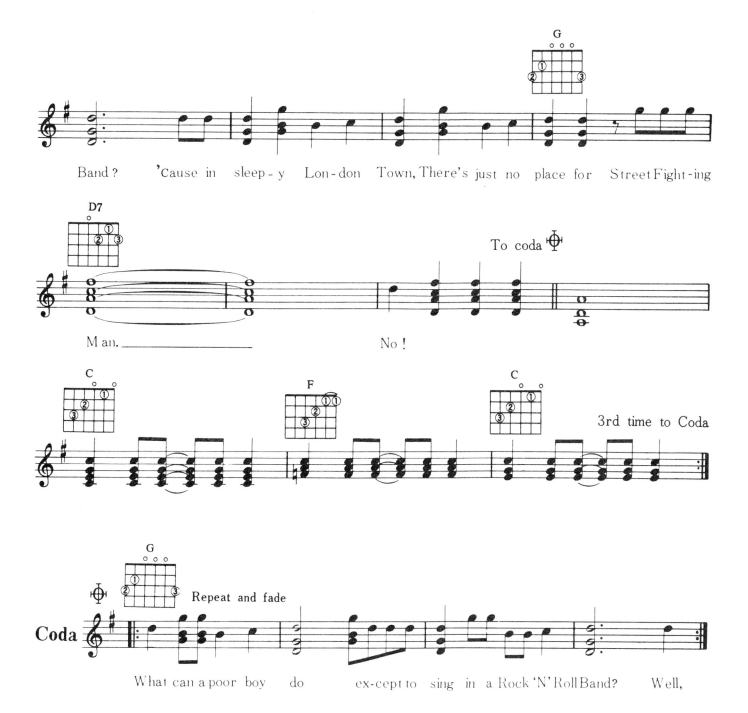

Band?   'Cause in sleep-y Lon-don Town, There's just no place for Street Fight-ing

Man._____   No!

3rd time to Coda

Coda   Repeat and fade

What can a poor boy   do   ex-cept to sing in a Rock 'N' Roll Band?   Well,

2. Hey! Think the time is right for a Palace Revolution.
    But where I live the game to play is Compromise Solution!
    Well, Then what can a poor boy do except to sing for a Rock 'N' Roll band?
    'Cause in sleepy London Town there's just no place for Street Fighting Man!

3. Hey! Said my name is called Disturbance I'll shout and scream,
    I'll kill the king I'll rail at all his servants.
    Well what can a poor boy do except to sing for a rock 'n' roll band?
    'Cause in sleepy London town there's just no place for Street Fighting Man.

Sweet And Lovely

Words & Music by Gus Arnheim, Harry Tobias & Jules Lemare

Suggested registration: violin (1), Rhythm: string quartet (fingered auto accompaniment)

2. Skies above me never were as blue as her eyes.
   And she loves me. Who would want a sweeter surprise?

179

What To Do

Words and Music by Mick Jagger and Keith Richards

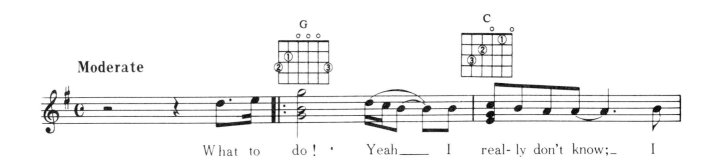

What to do! Yeah___ I real-ly don't know;_ I

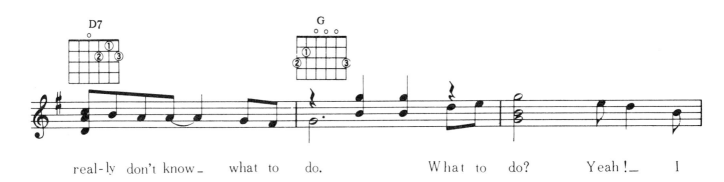

real-ly don't know_ what to do. What to do? Yeah!_ I

real-ly don't know;_ I real-ly don't know_

May-be when the
There's a place where
Hur-ry peo-ple, get

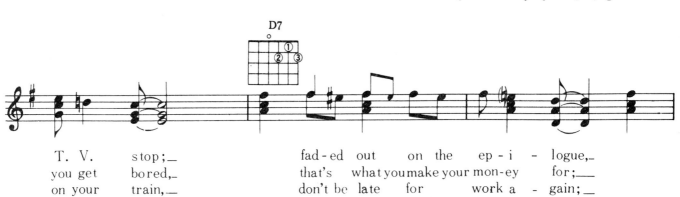

T. V. stop;_ fad-ed out on the ep-i - logue,_
you get bored, that's what you make your mon-ey for;_
on your train,_ don't be late for work a - gain;_

watch the screen just fade a - way;_ no I real - ly don't know,_ I
drink and dance to four o - 'clock,_ now you real - ly don't know,_ you
I think it's time to go to bed;_ no I real - ly don't know,_ I

real-ly don't know __ what to do. Yeah, noth-ing to do, __ no-where to go,_
real-ly don't know __ what to

__ you're talk-ing, to peo - ple that you don't know;_ there's n - n - n - noth-

- ing to do, do, do,_ no, you real-ly don't know,_ you really don't know _ what to

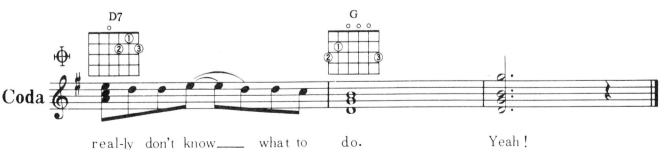

real-ly don't know __ what to do. Yeah!

The Poor People Of Paris (La Goualante Du Pauvre Jean)

Words & Music by Marguerite Monnot & R. Rouzaud

Suggested registration: whistle, Rhythm: march (2) (fingered auto accompaniment)

out;   out of there with –

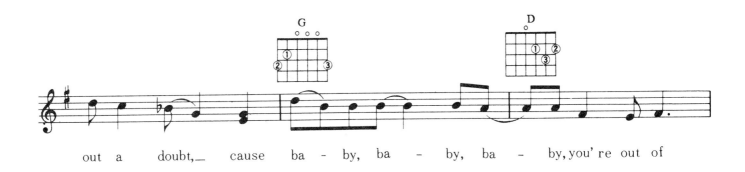

out a   doubt, —   cause ba - by, ba - by, ba - by, you're out of

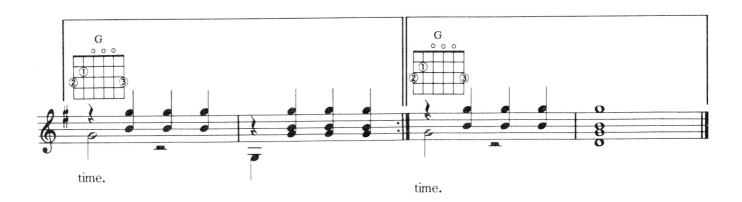

time.   time.

2. A girl who wants to run away
    Discovers that she's had her day;
    It's no good you thinking that you are still mine.
    You're out of touch my baby, my poor unfaithful baby,
    I said baby, baby, baby, you're out of time.

3. You thought   you were a clever girl
    Giving up your social whirl;
    But you can't come back and be the first in line.
    You're so obsolete my baby, my poor old fashioned baby ,
    I said baby, baby, baby, you're out of time.

I Am The Walrus
Words and music by John Lennon and Paul McCartney

al - ways some - thing there___ to re-mind me.

to Coda ⊕

1. **2.**

I was born to

love you___ and I will nev - er be free, you'll al-ways be a

D.C. al Coda

part of me,___ wo,___ wo,___ wo.___

⊕ **Coda**

I was born to love you___ and I will

186

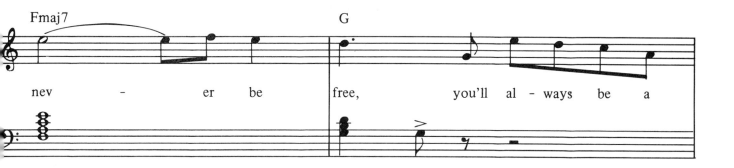

nev - er be free, you'll al - ways be a

part of me. ___ ___ There is al - ways some - thing there___

repeat to fade

___ to re - mind me.

2. When shadows fall, I pass the small cafe where
   we would dance at night;
   And I can't help re - calling how it felt to
   kiss and hold you tight.

3. If you should find you miss the sweet and tender
   love we used to share;
   Just come back to the places where we used to
   go and I'll be there.

All My Loving

Words and music by John Lennon and Paul McCartney

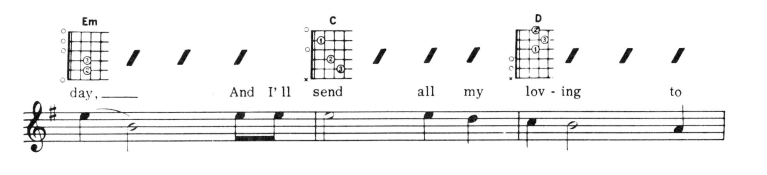

day, _____ And I'll send all my lov - ing to

(No Chord)

you. _____ All my lov - ing

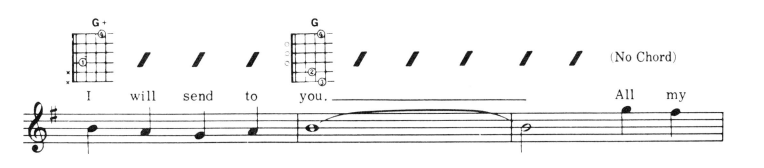

(No Chord)

I will send to you. _____ All my

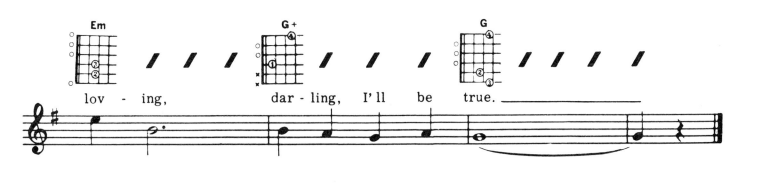

lov - ing, dar - ling, I'll be true. _____

The Twelfth Of Never

Words by Paul Francis Webster Music by Jerry Livingston

Suggested registration: violin (2), Rhythm: country (fingered auto accompaniment)

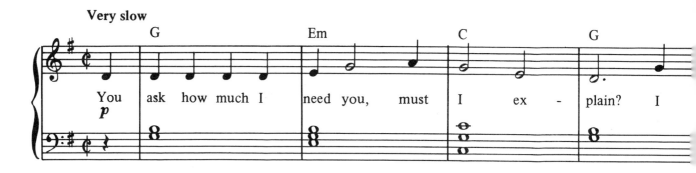

You ask how much I need you, must I ex - plain? I

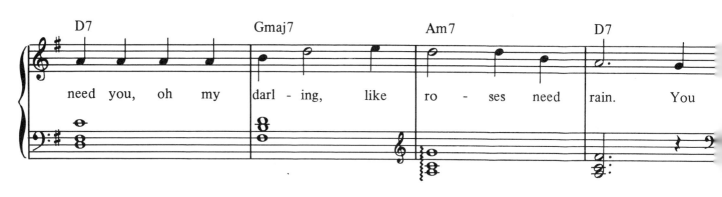

need you, oh my darl - ing, like ro - ses need rain. You

ask how long I'll love you, I'll tell you true, un -

til the Twelfth of Nev - er, I'll still be lov - ing you.

Hold me close, nev - er let me go. Hold me

I'm A Loser
Words and music by John Lennon and Paul McCartney

I should have known__ she would win in the
end. I'm a los - er, and I lost some-one who's
near to me, I'm a los - er, and I'm
not what I ap - pear to be.__ pear to be.__

2. Although I laugh
   And I act like a clown
   Beneath this mask
   I am wearing a frown.

   My tears are falling
   Like rain from the sky
   Is it for her
   Or myself that I cry.

   I'm a loser
   And I lost someone who's near to me
   I'm a loser
   And I'm not what I appear to be.

3. What have I done
   To deserve such a fate
   I realize
   I have left it too late.

   And so it's true
   Pride comes before a fall
   I'm telling you
   So that you won't lose all

   I'm a loser *(etc.)*

Back In The USSR

Words and music by John Lennon and Paul McCartney

pack my case   Hon- ey, dis- con- nect the phone.
ring - ing out,   Come and keep your com- rade warm. } I'm back in the U. S. S. R.,

You don't know how luck- y   you   are, boy.   Back   in   the   U. S.,

(No chord _____

_____)   back   in the   U. S.,   back in   the   U. S. S.   R.   Well, the

U- kraine girls real- ly   knock me out, they   leave the   West be - hind.   And

Mos- cow girls make me   sing and shout _   that Geor- gia's al- ways on my mi - mi -

mi- mi- mi- mi- mi- mi mind. _____   Back   in the   U. S. S. R.,   Oh,   yeah.

D.S.   al ⊕ Coda

195

Don't Let Me Down

Words and music by John Lennon and Paul McCartney

do me, yes, she does.
done me, she done me good.

Don't let me down,

Don't let me down, ___ don't let me down, ___

don't let me down. ___ I'm in love for the first time,

don't you know it's gon-na last. It's a love that lasts for-

ev-er, it's a love that had no past. No chords *D.C. al ⊕ Coda*

⊕ *Coda*

(*hold*)

She Loves You

Words and music by John Lennon and Paul McCartney

1. You think you lost your love, well, I
2. (She) said you lost hurt her so, she
3. (You) know it's up to you I

saw her yes - ter - day - yi - yah, it's you she's think - ing
al - most lost her mind, and now she says she
think it's on - ly fair, pride can hurt you

of, and she told me what to say - yi - yay. She says she
knows, you're not the hurt - ing kind. She says she
too. A - pol - o - gize to her. Be - cause she

loves you and you know that can't be bad. _____

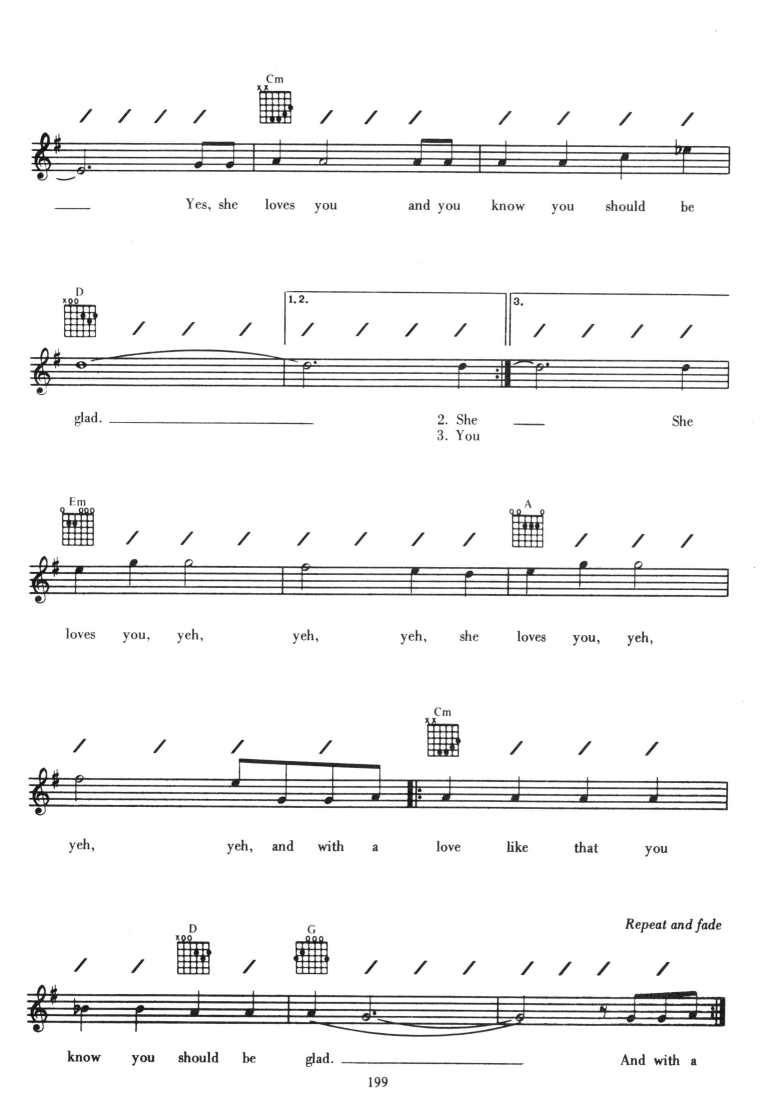

Cm

Yes, she loves you and you know you should be

D

1.2.   3.

glad. _____   2. She ___ She
                            3. You

Em   A

loves you, yeh, yeh, yeh, she loves you, yeh,

Cm

yeh, yeh, and with a love like that you

Repeat and fade

D   G

know you should be glad. _____   And with a

199

Can't Buy Me Love

Words and music by John Lennon and Paul McCartney

201

Eight Days A Week
Words and music by John Lennon and Paul McCartney

ain't got noth-in' but love, babe,
ain't got noth-in' but love, girl, Eight days a

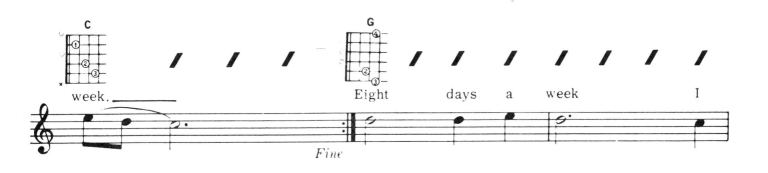

week._____ Eight days a week I

Fine

love_____ you.___ Eight days a

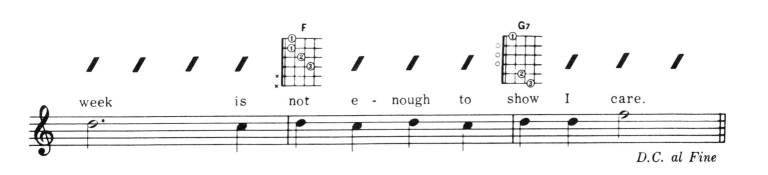

week is not e-nough to show I care.

D.C. al Fine

Ticket To Ride

Words and music by John Lennon and Paul McCartney

I don't know why she's rid - ing so high ___ She ought to
think right she ought to do right by me. Be -
fore she gets to say - ing good - bye, ___ She ought to
think right, she ought to do right by me.

D.C. al Coda

ride, but she don't care, My ba - by don't care.

Repeat and Fade

I'm Looking Through You

Words and music by John Lennon and Paul McCartney

3. Your thinking of me in the same old way.
You were above me, but not today.
The only difference is you're down there;
I'm looking through you, and you're nowhere.

Don't Go Breaking My Heart
Words and music by Ann Orson and Carte Blanche

BOY: So don't go break-ing my heart ____

____ GIRL: I won't go break-ing your heart ____

BOTH: Don't go break-ing my heart ____

D.%. al Coda

⊕ *CODA*

____ BOTH: Don't go break-ing my, don't go break-ing my,

to fade ad lib.

1,5 don't go break-ing my heart ____ GIRL: I won't go break-ing your heart. ____

2,3,4

Nobody Does It Better

Words and music by Carole Bayer Sager and Marvin Hamlisch

*Tune 6th string to D

but some-how you found me. I tried to hide from your

when-ev-er you hold me. There's some kind of mag - ic in -

love light, But like heav - en a - bove me

side you That keeps me from run - nin'

the spy who loved me is keep - in' all my se - crets safe to -

but just keep it com - in' how'd you learn to do the things you

1.
night.

2.
do? And

D. S. al Coda

Coda
Ba - by, ba - by,

(no chords)

ba - by you're the best.

fingering as before

Fire And Rain

Words and music by James Taylor

Slow rock

1. Just yes-ter-day morn-in' they let me know you were gone, __

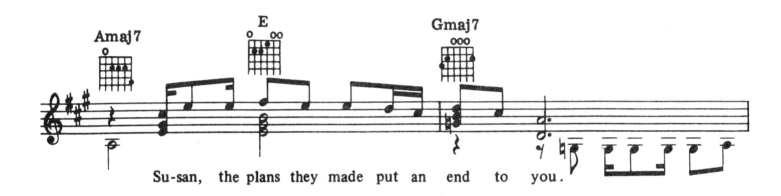

Su-san, the plans they made put an end to you.

I walked out this morn - in' and I wrote down this song, __

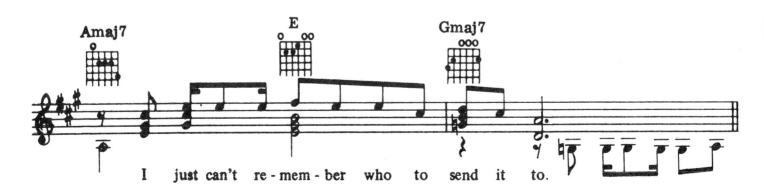

I just can't re - mem - ber who to send it to.

Chorus:

I've seen fire and I've seen rain, I seen sun-ny days_ that I thought would nev-er end, I seen lone-ly times_ when I could not find a friend,_ But I al-ways thought that I'd see you a-gain._

2. Won't you look down upon me, Jesus, you got to help me make a stand
   You just got to see me through another day
   My body's achin' and my time is at hand
   An' I won't make it any other way. *(Chorus)*

3. Been walkin' my mind to an easy time, my back turned towards the sun
   Lord knows when the cold wind blows it'll turn your head around
   Well, there's hours of time on the telephone line, to talk about things to come
   Sweet dreams and flying machines in pieces on the ground. *(Chorus)*

Run To You

Words and music by Adams/Vallance

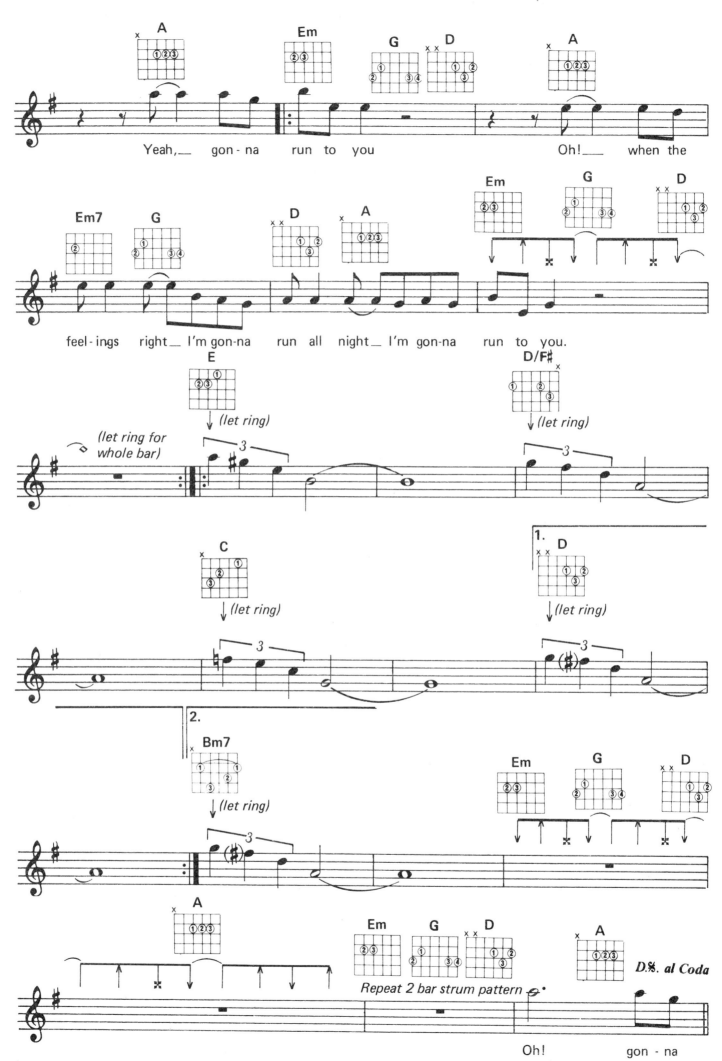

Yeah,__ gon-na run to you   Oh!__ when the

feel-ings right__ I'm gon-na run all night__ I'm gon-na run to you.

Repeat 2 bar strum pattern

Oh!   gon - na

VERSE 2:
She's got a heart of gold,
She'd never let me down.
But you're the one that always turns me on
And keep me comin' round.
I know her love is true,
But it's so damn easy makin' love to you.
I got my mind made up
I need to feel your touch.
    (To Chorus)

The Sun Always Shines On TV

Words and music by Pal Waaktaar

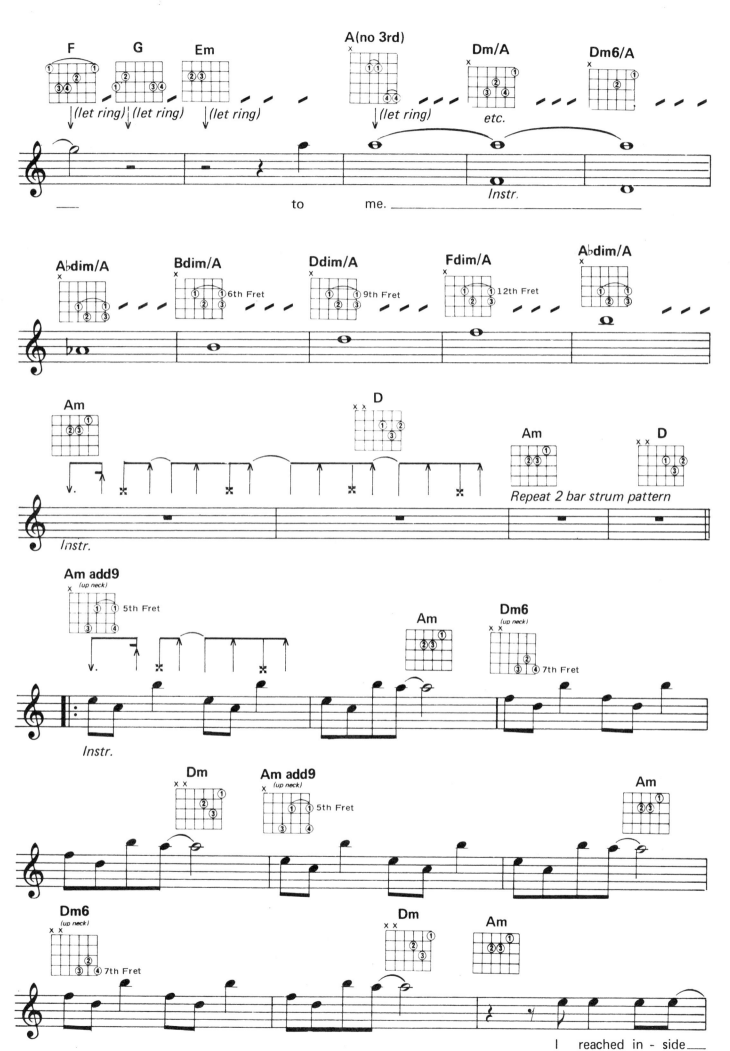

VERSE 2:
Please don't ask me to defend
The shameful lowlands of the way I'm drifting
Gloomily through time.
I reached inside myself today
Thinking there's got to be some way
To keep my troubles distant.

221

Breaking Up Is Hard To Do

Words and music by Neil Sedaka and Howard Greenfield

You tell me that you're leav - in', I can't be - lieve it's

true! Girl, there's just no liv - in' with-out ____

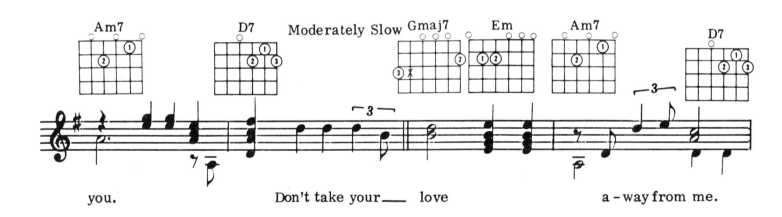

you. Don't take your ____ love a-way from me.

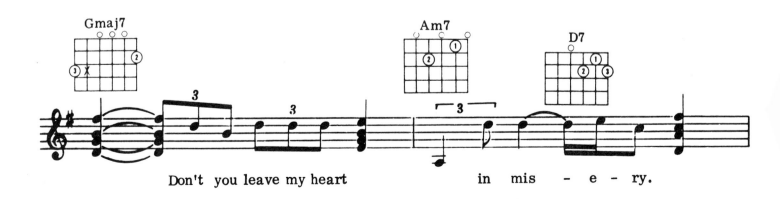

Don't you leave my heart in mis - e - ry.

'Cause if you go, _____ then I'll ___ be blue, ___

break - in' up ___ is hard ___ to do. Re - mem - ber

when _____ you held me tight, and you kissed me

all through___ the night?___ Think of all ___

that we ___ been through, _____ and break-in' up is hard_____ to do.___

223

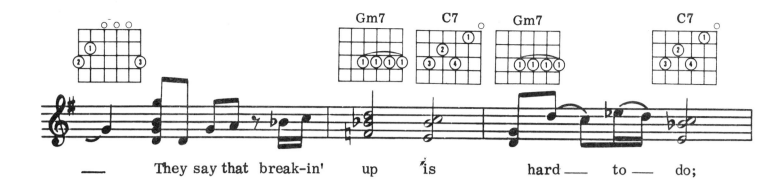

They say that break-in' up is hard — to — do;

now I know, ___ I know ___ that it's true. ___

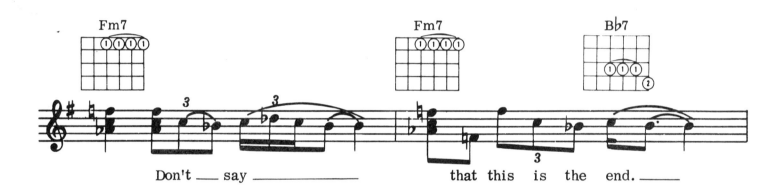

Don't ___ say _____ that this is the end. ___

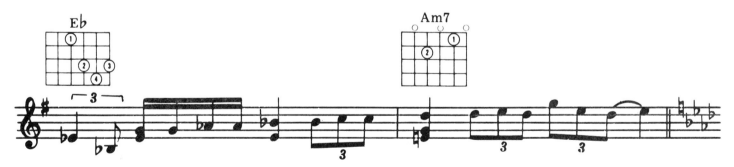

In-stead of break-in' up, I wish that we were mak-in' up a-gain. ___

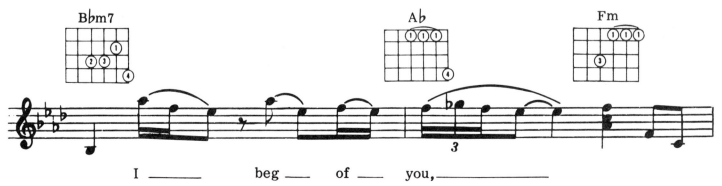

I ___ beg ___ of ___ you, _____

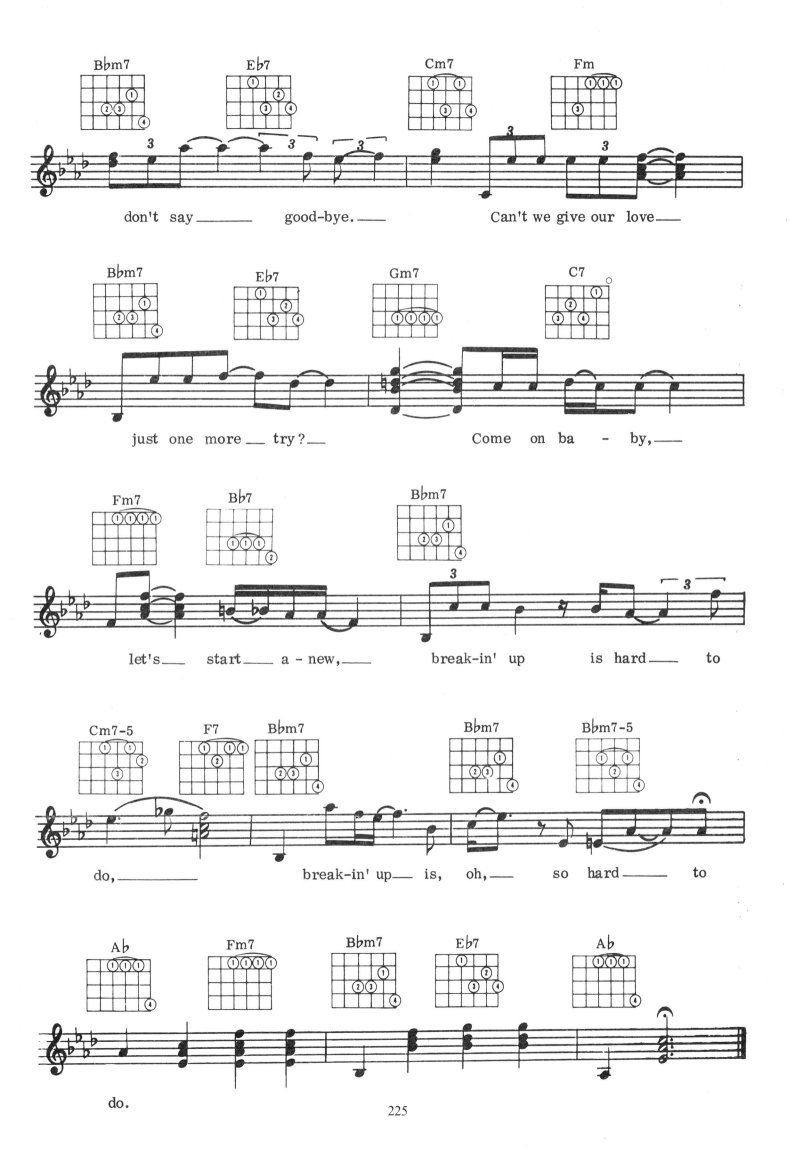

Instant Karma
Words and music by John Lennon

Moderately

In - stant Kar - ma's gon - na get you,
In - stant Kar - ma's gon - na get you,

gon - na knock you right on the head! ___
gon - na knock you right in the face! ___

You bet - ter get your - self to - geth - er.
You bet - ter get your - self to - geth - er.

Pret - ty soon you're gon-na be dead! What in the world you think-ing
Join the hu - man race! How in the world you gon - na

of?—   Laugh-in' in the face of love,—
see?—   Laugh-in' at ___ fools like me,—

C   D

what on earth you tryin' to   do?   It's   up to you!   Yeah
who on earth d'you think you   are?   A   su-per star?   Well, al-

1.   **2.**   %

E7   E7   G   Bm   Em

you!   right you are! Well we all   shine   on —   like the

G   Bm   Em   G   Bm

moon and the stars and the   sun!__   Yeh, we all   shine

Em   D   E7

D.S. for fade

on, ___   ev-'ry-one,   come on!

Maybe I'm Amazed

Words and music by Paul McCartney

Maybe I'm amazed at the way you're with me all the time,
And maybe I'm afraid of the way I need you.
Maybe I'm amazed at the way you help me sing my song,
  right me when I'm wrong,
And maybe I'm amazed at the way I really need you.

Just The Way You Are
Words and music by Billy Joel

good   times, ___   I'll   take   the   bad   times, ___
some - one ___   that   I   can   talk   to, ___
love   you, ___   an - y   bet - ter, ___

I'll   take   you   just   the   way ___   you
I   want   you   just   the   way ___   you
I   love   you   just   the   way ___   you

are.

To next strain

are.

Fine

are.

I   need   to   know   that   you   will   al   -   ways

be   the   same   old   some - one   that   I

knew.   Oh,   What   will   it

take   till   you   be - lieve   in   me

the   way   that   I   be - lieve   in   you?   I____

Piano Man
Words and music by Billy Joel

1. It's nine o - clock on a Sat - ur - day,
2. (Now) John at the bar is a friend of mine,
3. (Now) Paul is a real es - tate nov - el - ist,
4. (It's a) pret - ty good crowd for a Sat - ur - day,

The reg - u - lar crowd shuf - fles in
He gets me my drinks for free,
Who nev - er had time for a wife
And the man - ag - er gives me a smile

There's an old man sit - ting next to me
And he's quick with a joke or to light up your
And he's talk - in' with Da - vy who's still in the
'Cause he knows that it's me they've been com - in' to

Mak - in' love to his ton - ic and gin.
smoke But there's some - place that he'd rath - er be.
na - vy And prob - a - bly will be for life.
see To for - get a - bout life for a while.

He says, "Son, can you
He says, "Bill, I be -
And the wait - ress is
And the pia - no

play me a mem- o - ry?
lieve this is kill - ing me,"
prac - tic - ing pol - i - tics,
sounds like a car - ni - val

I'm not real - ly
As a smile ran a -
As the bus - 'ness - men
And the mi - cro - phone

sure how it goes,
way from his face
slow - ly get stoned
smells like a beer

But it's sad and it's
"Well, I'm sure that I
Yes, they're shar - ing a
And they sit at the

sweet and I knew it com — plete
could be a mov - ie star
drink they call lone - li - ness
bar and put bread in my jar

When I wore a
If I could get
But it's bet - ter than
And say, "Man, what are

235

young - er man's clothes."
out   of   this   place."
drink - in' a - lone.
you   do - in'   here?"

Da   da   da—
Da   da   da—
Instrumental_____
Da   da   da—

___   de   de   da_____   da   da—
___   de   de   da_____   da   da—
___   de   de   da_____   da   da—

___   de   de   da   da   da—
___   de   de   da   da   da—
___   de   de   da   da   da—

Sing   us   a   song, you're   the   pia - no   man—

236

Sing us a song to - night   Well, we're

all in the mood for a mel - o - dy,   And you've got us

feel - in' al - right.

2. Now
3. Now
4. It's a

Candle In The Wind

Words and music by Elton John and Bernie Taupin

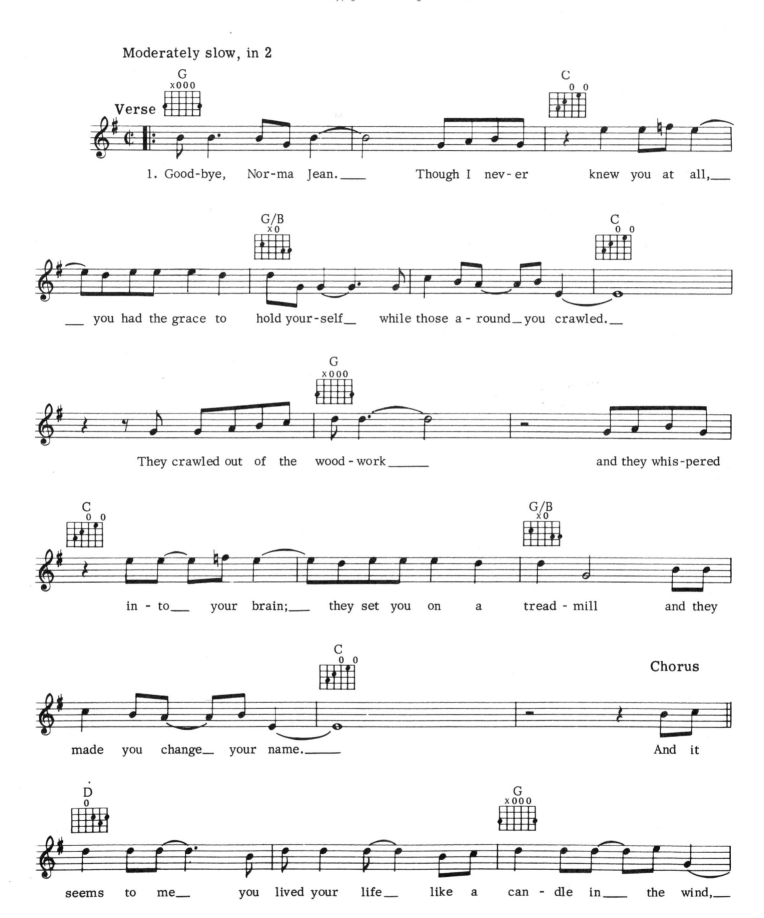

nev - er know - ing who to cling to when the rain set in.___ And I would have liked___ to have known you, but I was just a kid.___ Your can - dle burned___ out long be - fore___ your leg - end ev - er did._____

1. 2. | 3.
Your can - dle burned___ out long be - fore___ your leg - end ev - er did.____

2. Loneliness was tough, the toughest role you ever played;
Hollywood created a superstar and pain was the price you paid.
Even when you died the press still hounded you;
All the papers had to say was that Marilyn was found in the nude.

(Chorus)

3. Goodbye, Norma Jean. Though I never knew you at all,
You had the grace to hold yourself while those around you crawled.
Goodbye, Norma Jean, from the young man in the twenty-second row
Who sees you as something more than sexual, more than just our Marilyn Monroe.

(Chorus)

Maybe Baby
Words and music by Charles Hardin and Norman Petty

Moderato, with a steady beat

Well, you are the one that makes me sad, ____

And you are the one that makes me glad, ___ when some-day you _

___ want me, ___ I'll be there, wait and see. Oh,

May-be, Ba-by, I'll have you, _____ May-be, Ba-by,

you'll be true, _____ May-be, Ba-by, I'll have you __ for

me. ____ ____ me. ____ ____

It's So Easy
Words and music by Buddy Holly and Norman Petty

Moderately bright (good beat)

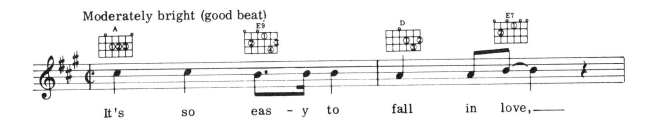

It's so eas-y to fall in love, _____

It's so eas-y to _____ fall _____ in love. _____

VERSE 1

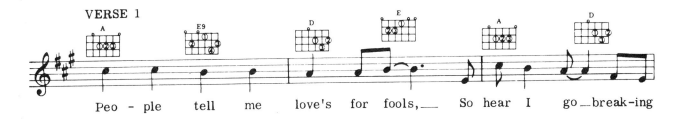

Peo-ple tell me love's for fools, _____ So hear I go _____ break-ing

CHORUS

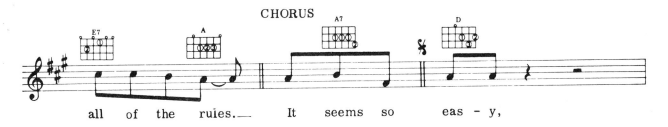

all of the rules. _____ It seems so eas-y,

so dog-gone eas-y;

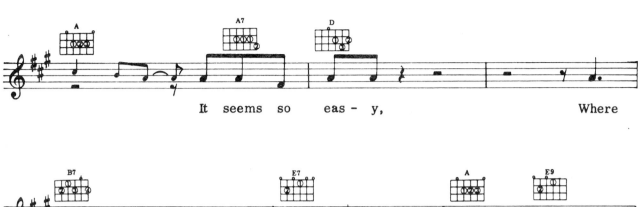

It seems so eas - y, Where

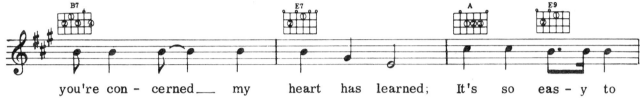

you're con - cerned__ my heart has learned; It's so eas - y to

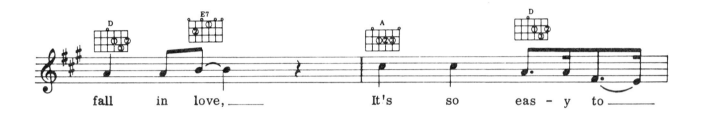

fall in love, ____ It's so eas - y to ____

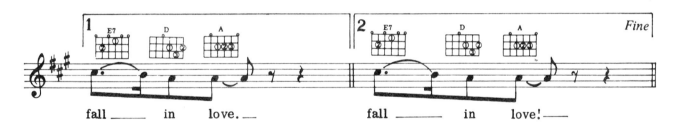

1 fall ____ in love. ____ **2** fall ____ in love! ____ *Fine*

VERSE 2

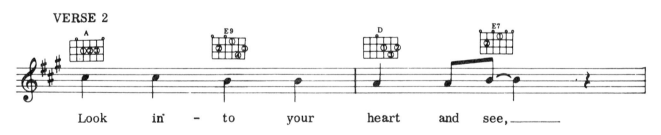

Look in' - to your heart and see, ____

D.S. al Fine

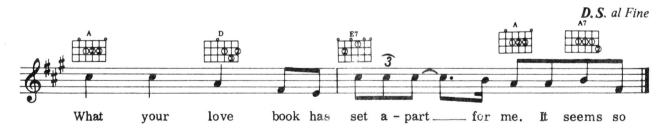

What your love book has set a - part____ for me. It seems so

243

Peggy Sue Got Married
Words and music by Buddy Holly

You re - call the girl __ that's been in near - ly ev - 'ry song; __

This is what __ I heard, of course the sto - ry could be wrong;

She's the one, __ I've been told, That she's wear-in' a band __

__ of __ gold; Peg-gy Sue __ got mar - ried not long a - go.

Peg-gy sue got mar - ried not long a - go. _____

Oh Boy
Words and music by Sunny West, Bill Tilghman and Norman Petty

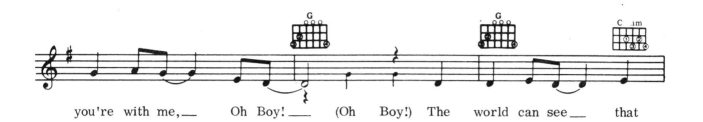

you're with me, ___ Oh Boy! ___ (Oh Boy!) The world can see ___ that

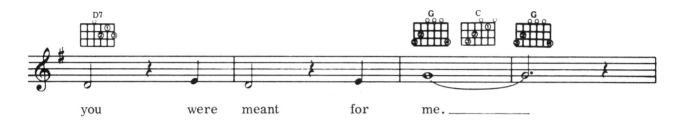

you were meant for me. _____

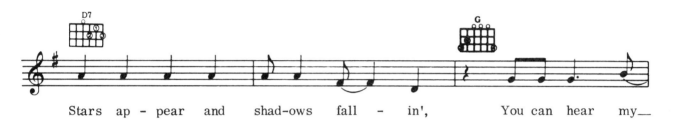

Stars ap - pear and shad-ows fall - in', You can hear my ___

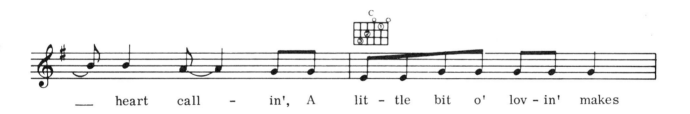

___ heart call - in', A lit - tle bit o' lov - in' makes

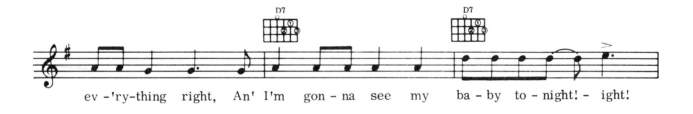

ev -'ry-thing right, An' I'm gon - na see my ba - by to - night! - ight!

All o' my love, all o' my kiss-in', You don't know what

you been miss - in'. Oh Boy!__ (Oh Boy!) When you're with me,__ Oh Boy!

__ (Oh Boy!) The world can see__ that you were meant for

(To interlude) *Fine*

me. __ me. __

INTERLUDE

Dum   de dum dum,   Oh Boy!   Dum   de dum dum,   Oh Boy!

Ah, _____   Ah, _____

D S al Fine

Ah, _____   Ah. _____

You Can't Always Get What You Want

Words & Music by Mick Jagger & Keith Richards

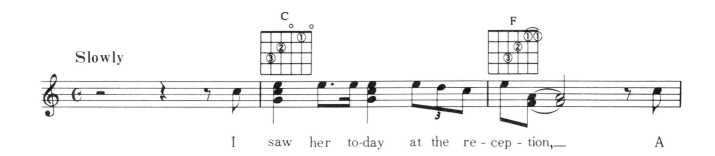

Slowly

I saw her to-day at the re - cep - tion,___ A

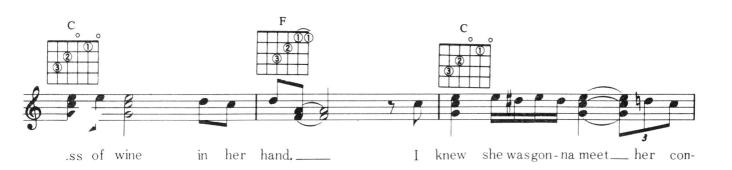

.ss of wine in her hand.___ I knew she was gon - na meet___ her con-

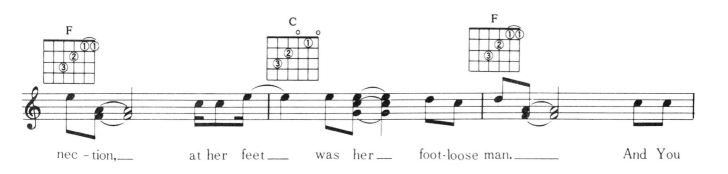

nec - tion,___ at her feet___ was her___ foot-loose man._____ And You

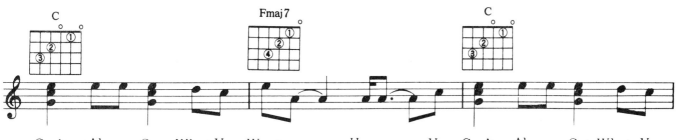

Can't Al-ways Get What You Want_____ Hon-ey,___ You Can't Al-ways Get What You

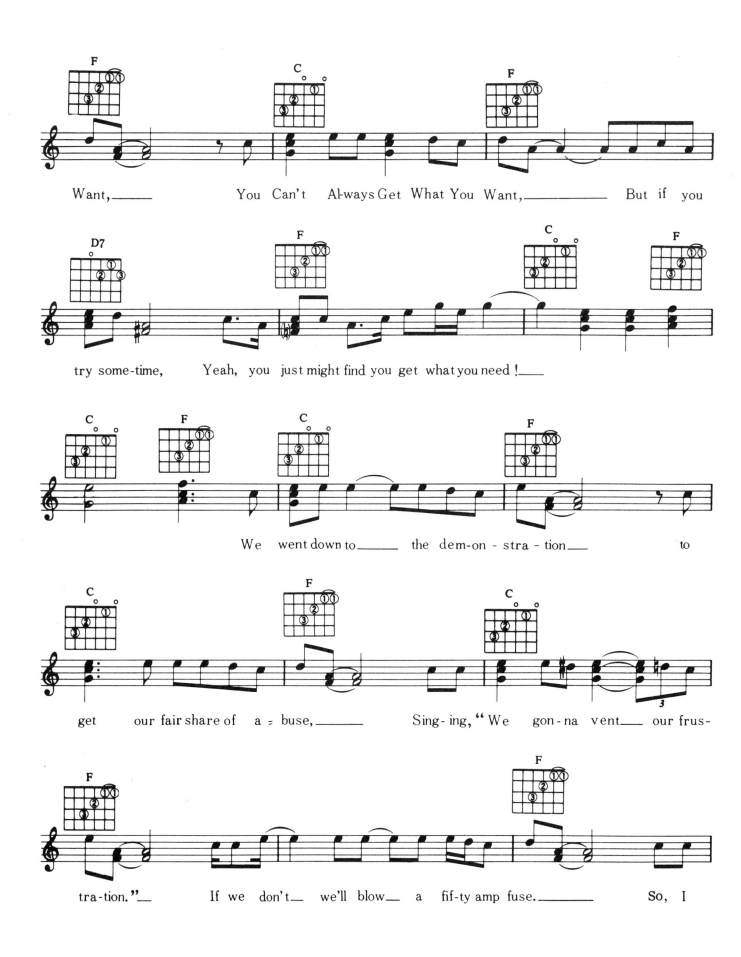

Want,_____ You Can't Always Get What You Want,_____ But if you

try some-time, Yeah, you just might find you get what you need !___

We went down to_____ the dem-on - stra - tion___ to

get our fair share of a = buse,_____ Sing-ing, "We gon-na vent___ our frus-

tra-tion."___ If we don't___ we'll blow___ a fif-ty amp fuse._____ So, I

went to the Chelsea Drug - store___ to get your_____ pre-scrip-tion

filled._____ I was stand-ing in line _____ with your friend Jim-my.____ And

man, did he look_ pret-ty ill._____ We de-cid-ed that we would have a so-

- da,___ My fav'-rite fla-vor___ was cher-ry red._____ I

sing this song___ to my friend, Jim-my,___ And he said_ one word to me and that was

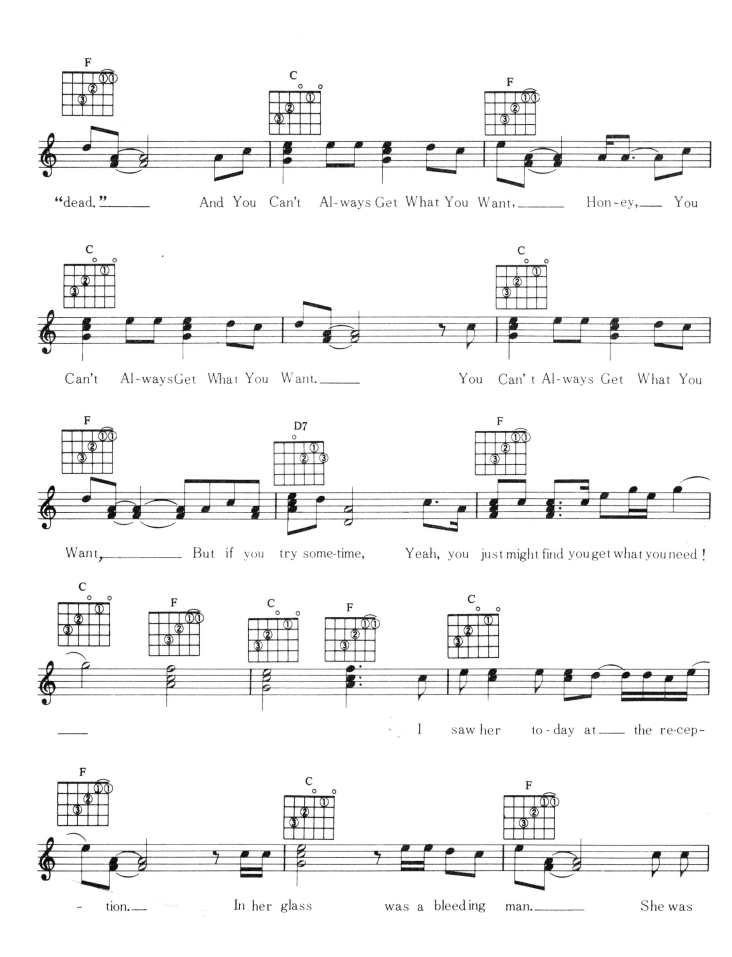

"dead." ___ And You Can't Al-ways Get What You Want, ___ Hon-ey,___ You

Can't Al-waysGet What You Want.___ You Can't Al-ways Get What You

Want,___ But if you try some-time, Yeah, you just might find you get what you need !

___ I saw her to-day at ___ the re-cep-

- tion.___ In her glass was a bleed ing man.___ She was

prac-tised at the art____ of de-cep-tion;____ I could tell by her blood - stained____

hands.____ And you Can't Always Get What You Want,____ Hon-ey,___ You

Can't Al-ways Get What You Want.____ You Can't Al-ways Get What You

Want,_____ But if you try some-time, Yeah, you just might find you get what you need!

1. ____

And You ____

253

Your Song
Words and music by Elton John and Bernie Taupin

Moderately

live.   you.

And you_ can tell ev - 'ry - bod - y   this_ is {your / the} song._

It may_ be quite_ sim - ple but_

now that it's done, _____   I hope you don't mind,_

I hope you don't mind _____ that I put _ down in

255

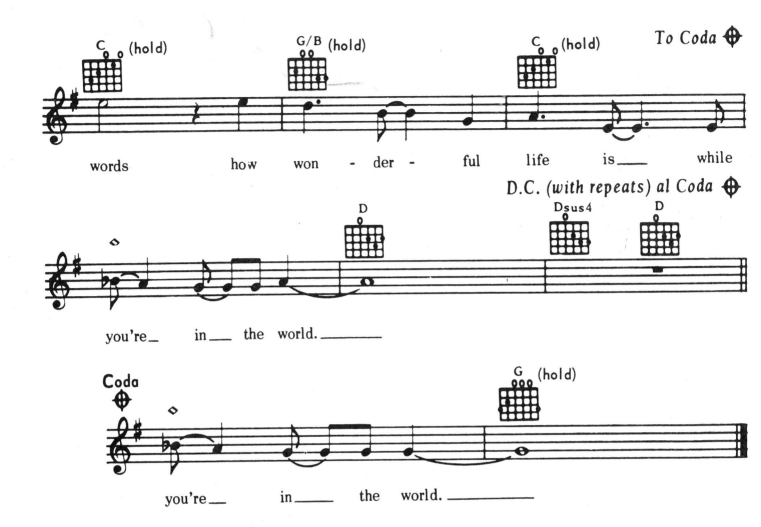

To Coda ⊕

words   how   won - der - ful   life   is___   while

D.C. (with repeats) al Coda ⊕

you're__   in__ the world._____

Coda
⊕

you're__   in___ the   world._____

2. If I was a sculptor, but then again no,
   Or a man who makes potions in a travelin' show,
   I know it's not much but it's the best I can do,
   My gift is my song and this one's for you.
   (Chorus)

3. I sat on the roof and kicked off the moss,
   Well a few of the verses, well they've got me quite cross,
   But the sun's been quite kind while I wrote this song,
   It's for people like you that keep it turned on.

4. So excuse me forgetting, but these days I do,
   You see I've forgotten if they're green or they're blue,
   Anyway, the thing is, what I really mean,
   Yours are the sweetest eyes I've ever seen.
   (Chorus)

Printed in Malta by Progress Press Co. Ltd   1/09 (168083)